Fairy Tales Come True!

John McGregor B.A.

John McGregor

GREGALACH BOOKS

**Front cover picture is of the author in 2011 on
Portsdown Hill with Thorney Island in the background**

First Edition published in 2015

Copyright © 2015 John McGregor

Gregalach books

John McGregor

All rights reserved.

ISBN-10:1508497168

ISBN-13:9781508497165

'The McGregors, despite them, shall flourish forever'.

John McGregor

DEDICATION

This book is dedicated to all the lads from Hercules First Line, 242 OCU, Royal Air Force Thorney Island who shaped my life - probably much more than they realized!

FOREWORD BY BOB JOHNSON.

This book is the long-awaited sequel to John McGregor's highly successful 'Fairy Tales of an SAC' which provided an entertaining and unexpected insight into his world of the RAF during the late sixties. Mac's hilarious tales of his exploits and his colleagues during that era have brought many of those back in touch today as a result of the book, enjoying annual reunions as a result.

Now John has brought his lads and lasses right up to date – what had they all been doing, how are they today? What did they think of his book, what memories did it spark of those great days? This light-hearted romp answers all those questions, and more. It's a great read, not only for ex-service personnel but also for anyone who enjoys a good tale, well told of what life was really like 'On Her Majesty's Service'.

PREFACE

When I left The Royal Air Force in 1972, a little part of me stayed behind at Thorney island. Over the next 37 years I went in a completely different direction work-wise, got married, had children and got on with life. But I always carried the people, the stories and my memories of Thorney with me as I went, because one day I wanted to write it all down, to see if I could tell it how it was. In 2009 I finally did it, but I was totally unprepared for the journey is has taken me on since then: renewed old friendships, annual reunions, totally-unexpected developments and a lot more. Quite frankly, it has and still is blowing me away, and has added a new dimension to my life as I moved into my sixties – and I am excited, because I am sure there is much more to come...

INTRODUCTION

They don't tell you when you write a book, one that is about people, you should consider the fact that you just might meet up with them again. I didn't – and I did!

Fairy Tales Come True!

CONTENTS

1	They Never Tell You That...	17
2	Thorney Island	21
3	Original Book Comments	28
4	Fifteen Minutes Of Fame	44
5	242 OCU	53
6	Fairy Tales of an SAC	59
7	Martin Shuker	66
8	Bring On The Twins	74
9	Julian	83
10	Hardy Here!	87

11	Bentley	Pg 92
12	Twinkle In Your Eye	Pg 99
13	Landing In Hot Water	Pg 102
14	Ron's Scams	Pg 107
15	Pete's Stories	Pg 113
16	Lads' Contributions	Pg 137
17	Those Who Got Away	Pg 154
18	'Owed' To Thorney Island	Pg 158

ACKNOWLEDGMENTS

This is to acknowledge the valuable contribution of the 'old' lads from 242 OCU who sent me comments about the original 'Fairy Tales of an SAC' and now contributions for this sequel 'Fairy Tales Come True!' both of which mean so very much to me.

Fairy Tales Come True

John McGregor

1. **They Never Tell You That...**

'That's nice, a queue now!' I thought smugly, as another person appeared to be standing in line, close behind the rather boring bloke I was talking to. It was only twenty minutes into my first-ever book signing at Waterstones in the lovely old town of Chichester, and I was feeling quite pleased with myself as I had already signed and sold two books. Shifting my position slightly to get a better view I looked straight into the eyes of a plumpish, middle-aged lady who stared back intently at me with a strange look on her face - and I thought 'Oh my God, it's Jill!'

Men can only do one thing at once, can't they? I tried to eke out the tedious interview with the older chappy from the RAF who was picking my brains (not usually a lengthy task) about writing his proposed book like-everyone-does, but at the same time my mind was racing, trying to remember what I had actually written about Jill in the book. From the look on her face it seemed as though I might have some explaining to do...

Jill was one of a bunch of female telephonists we young airmen had dated in the late sixties. The practice was, every month on a virtually all-male camp the authorities would send a free bus to either the local nurses home, teachers training college or similar female establishment to attend a monthly dance (discos hadn't quite started), and then for weeks, months and sometimes for ever we would be attached to such girls. The telephonists were, in my words 'a rum lot' as they used to listen in to phone calls from the rich and famous. Indeed in 'Fairy Tales of an SAC' (FTOAS from now on) I tell of one true story in the book about listening to the lead singer of probably the most famous rock band in the world, still Rolling along today, Stone me!

In my case Jill and I went out for a few months, but in the gang I hung around with the emphasis was on the 'Bumble Bee' syndrome, i.e. flitting from flower to flower restlessly, distributing pollen wherever possible – I'm sure you catch my drift. In the book I described Jill as 'petite, dark and attractive' – phew! But in addition, just to spice it up a bit, I also described her as a little 'staid' and said that she still lived with her parents. But in those days I wasn't into long relationships and wanted to move on. I had decided to end it one night, but before I could we were involved in a car accident and ended up in hospital together.

While being stitched up I saw Jill's notes, and was surprised to find out she was twenty-nine, although she had told me she was twenty-four. I was also lying, as I was twenty and told her I was twenty-four! Although I took some flowers and chocolates round to her house the next day, I knew this was it, and I wouldn't be contacting her again, though I told her I would ring her – and didn't. There's more to the story, so if you don't know and want to you'll have to get a copy of FTOAS (it's well worth it).

Back at Waterstones my wannabe author slipped away, and Jill stepped smartly forward. I notice she was clutching a well-thumbed copy of my book in her hand, and I wondered if she was going to ask me to sign it - or hit me with it.

'Hello, John,' she started, through clenched teeth. 'I don't suppose you remember this 'old maid' do you? You remember, the 'staid' one, who still lived with her Mum and Dad?'

'Ha, ha! Of course I do, Jill,' I chuckled nervously, giving her a peck on the cheek. 'How could I forget? How are you?'

'And this is my husband, Peter.' Why are their men always seven foot three? I swung round to see a large, serious-looking man staring coldly down to me. He looked as though he'd been thrown out of the Gestapo for cruelty, glaring down at me through knotted eyebrows as if about to deliver the death sentence. We shook hands grudgingly and Jill and I began to chat about what had happened during those eventful times from so long ago. An old friend of hers from the telephone exchange had read the book article in the Chichester Observer, rang Jill up and said:

'Hey, you remember that young airman you dated in the sixties? Well, he's written a book, I bought a copy – and you're in it!'

We discussed our mutual friends from that era and soon Jill began to thaw out. After what seemed like two hours, but was probably only ten minutes, an old familiar male face appeared and I gratefully acknowledged him. Jill noted that and summarised:

'Well, John, it's been great to see you again - you little bugger! Now I hope you're going to sign my book for me?'

'Of course I am, Jill: it'll be a pleasure,' I gushed.

'And I hope you're going to write something nice!' she added. Well, I was hardly likely to risk any more trouble, was I, so I wrote: 'To Jill - how lovely to see you again after all these years. All the very best in life, yours very sincerely, John xxx'.

So Jill and I parted as friends, but the incident really threw me at the time. I certainly wasn't prepared for such events – and really should have been, it was to be the first of many. The incident taught me the valuable lesson that if you are going to write about anyone, then be prepared for the fact that you just might run into them again, and like me, have a little explaining to do. My only worry now is if I run into the bloke I described as a 'wanker' – well, he was – oh, and then there's the one whose petrol tank I weed in... Anyway, the good - no, make that the great news is that I've sold over 1,500 copies of FTOAS now, and have had some great fun since writing it - honest!

2. THORNEY ISLAND (or as some local girls called it - Horney Island!).

Thorney Island in the sun

Willed to me by the postings man

All my days I will sing in praise

Of your shining waters and long runways.

Apologies to Harry Belafonte and my mangled version of his 'Island In The Sun', but from about the middle of 1967 I had sung my little ditty I made up, initially in training to piss off all the southerners on my radio mechanics course at RAF Cosford. They had somewhat foolishly opted for bases in the south of the country on their 'Areas of Preference' list you filled in when in basic training. I remain convinced that devious forces are at work in the said postings department, and indeed as a Midlands boy who seemed certain to be sent to the V bomber bases of Lincolnshire I could hardly believe my luck when I was sent to Thorney Island. In truth I didn't even know where it was – but it sounded good. So I rubbed it in, like you do, especially with the Londoners sent to Ballykelly in Northern Ireland and Kinloss in north Scotland – awright lads?

Ever since landing in that heady, flower-power year of 1967 Thorney island has always held a very special place in my heart. It would seem it is the same for most of us who were posted to that idyllic place: everyone seems to have their own special memories of Thorney, and the strangest and most wonderful thing today is that the island hardly seems to have changed at all; how refreshing in these changeable days. Even the buildings are virtually the same, the airfield still seems to have that quiet serene atmosphere I always remember. If you are very lucky and actually live there, or nearby, you are truly blessed, and I count myself very fortunate to have spent four and a half years of my life at Thorney Island. Indeed, as far as the Royal Air Force is concerned it seems a place of many long stays, some people having served there on more than one occasion: what a posting!

Four years ago when Fairy Tales first came out, through his Police contacts Martin took me on a tour of Thorney. I had never been back since I left in 1972 and I was looking forward to the visit very much. I was blown away by the fact that the place was almost just as I remembered, we even naughtily drove round to the blocks and they looked exactly the same, although I imagine the rooms were individual now: I think it was six to a room during my last two years there. Yes, the garage blocks were there, where we illegally parked our cars until a snap inspection one day caught us out (see 'Lawbreakin' chapter in FTOAS), and so was the green area outside the block where we kicked a football round for hours. The mess building was just the same, and the window where we broke in to feed ourselves ('Cracking The Mess' chapter) late at night for a few months until – well, we didn't get caught that time, but nearly... The guardroom and SHQ looked exactly the same but as I had spent very little time in either, thankfully, as well as the main camp it all looked reassuringly comforting.

The Deeps Guard situation was a scream. I had written a chapter all about it in FTOAS chapter 13, see picture of the old one, circa 1970. I was curious to see what had happened to it. I fondly imagined that as it was under the army's control now the discipline and security would be markedly different. Were they? Well, yes and no... The reception building was a little bit more solidly built on the left hand side now, but the barrier was just the same. Instead of a miserable RAF Snowdrop or bored airman there was now a young pongo who looked about fourteen – although he had a gun!

Immediately prior to the first reunion, despite permission having been granted etc I thought I'd have a quick recce (see how my military training hadn't worn off?) and three days before the big day I journeyed alone up to the camp. I parked my car and explained to the sentry what was happening and he advised me to go into the office. Here I encountered a fairly scruffy corporal, aged about 30 I would guess. He was quite friendly, and when i explained why I was there, he picked up his clipboard and flipped through it.

'Saturday did you say? Well I haven't got anything here, but that doesn't mean anything. I'ts only Wednesday, I'm sure we'll get the info by then. What is it you're doing then?' I told him and he was fascinated.

'You were here in the sixties? Wow, did you enjoy it? What pubs did you use?' I realised at once he had 'Deeps Guard Syndrome', that built-in boredom that meant anything unusual helped to pass the time. We chatted for a while and his final comment sent me on my way blissfully happy.

'I'm on duty on Saturday, so don't worry about anything - I'll sort it out, I've got your mobile. I might even join you for a drink later!'. Perfect – nothing had changed, only the colour of the uniform – the security certainly hadn't! What a delightful place it still is. I understand Royal Air Force Thorney Island was built in the mid 1930s to strengthen Britain's defence – how glad am I that they did – and made a lovely job of it, one of my abiding memories is the pink and white blossom on all the trees thoughtfully planted everywhere.

To build on that experience, and after three successful reunions, last year Martin took me a long, four-hour walk right round the perimeter of the island. That was a great experience which I enjoyed very much. It was a lively day in May and we experienced just about all four seasons during the walk, although a lot of it was sunny – and that of course, is primarily how I will always remember Thorney Island - a wonderfully 'sunshiny' spot in the world. One of the great rewards, amongst many of our reunions is that we can enjoy the experience in the lovely Sailing Club, a place where I spent many happy hours during those halcyon days. That, again, has not changed at all, the building inside and outside is all just as I remembered. Yes, I should have learnt to sail at the time, one of life's regrets, but as I always say – there were so many other things to do at the time...

I understand that RAF Thorney Island closed as a station in 1976. By that time the 242 OCU resident and talented artist of the day, one Clive (Chalkie) Richardson had produced the pictured mural of a Hercules, and this was used in the formal closing ceremony of the station. I am indebted to Chalkie for the following picture and the information.

Although I am now lucky enough to live in sunny Spain, we get the English news and weather reports regularly, and as we all know Thorney Island shows up well on the UK maps that the TV weather forecast shows. In addition as you fly into the UK on an aircraft both to and from Gatwick you can usually see Thorney from the air - and do you know what? I still get goose bumps, and a huge nostalgic buzz when I see it below, the place means so much to me. Although it probably wasn't (yes it was), life always seemed so innocent in those days, before life got complicated with marriage, kids, mortgages and civilian life kicking in. At Thorney I was young, free and single (well, nearly) and in that cocooned station away from civvy street I had a wonderful time in my life.

When I left the RAF for good in 1972, I left part of me behind at Thorney, and through all my travels in life I regularly thought back and often fondly imagined I was still there. What is that expression about memories? Precious today, priceless tomorrow? The reunions mean that I am so lucky, I can still return every year, and get the same lurch in my stomach as I drive on to the island and see it all again: Deeps Guardroom, Married Quarters, the camp gates, SHQ, the guardroom, our mess and the blocks we lived in – all just the same. A naughty trip up the peri-track (don't tell anyone) shows what is now just a patch of green grass, with a little wooded area today where the Line Hut sat, where again we kicked a football around while we were waiting for something to happen – as we always were.

Four and a half years of anyone's life is a long time, and to me that period was a special time in my life, effectively going from boy to man, but perhaps without the responsibilities that came soon enough afterwards. In short it was idyllic: there must have been 'down' times, but I can't remember any. It seemed the sun always shone as I strolled to 'work' out of the block, over stiles either side of the cowfield and into the Line Hut. What fantastic memories…

3. ORIGINAL COMMENTS ON 'FAIRY TALES OF AN SAC'

Can you see how absorbed you get reading 'Fairy Tales of an SAC'?

When FTOAS came out in 2011 it provided delightful comments for me from all sorts of different directions. Here are some, and a very sincere thank you to all these contributors who were kind enough to share their impressions. I've put them in different sections:

From some who were there with me at the time (perhaps my main target, and source of the greatest pleasure to me...)

Damian (Al) Thomas:

'I have read your book... I have never laughed so much for a long time, it is all so just real, like yesterday. I read the first chapter and couldn't stop laughing - it was so "as it was", and typically you! I also read the reviews by your brother, and the journalist, they are good, so you should be very proud of your book. I have also read the part you sent to me, and like it a lot, it is just YOU....complete with the good parts, and not so good parts of YOUR life. A very easy and enjoyable read. My son, Stephen also read your book and he just couldn't believe those were the things we got up to. He rang me up several times laughing at various bits, and asking for more detail on what happened - I had to decline to enlighten him too much on some parts...lol!'

Graham Logg: (*unfortunately I havn't been able to encourage Graham to come to one of our reunions and I haven't heard from him for over a year, despite my efforts – but he did send me this review, and also some great photos, see in this book: ed Mac*).

'You asked me to give you my honest opinion on your book, so here it is------ close your eyes and think of pasties - but only Cornish ! How fascinating to read a book written by an "old" pal, relating to events, people and places that I knew so long ago! I thoroughly enjoyed it Mac, from beginning to end. You've awakened so many good, bad and "ugly" memories lying dormant in the old grey matter (now I might add, encased in a shiny "shell" with nothing between it and the sun!).

Cyprus fun skinny-dipping in the Med, circa 1970. Graham's the big bugger on the left, Tony Richardson in the middle, then me. Extreme left? No idea, anyone know?

Your own memory is obviously still in pretty good nick, Mac - mind you, it bloody well should be! Let's get down to some real nitty gritty here! If we use today's computer jargon in relation to your (definitely not slaving over hot coals) Thorney days, mate ---------swapping an odd radio box every couple of days, or even weeks is unlikely to even register on an atom-sized memory stick today! Unlike us poor fuggin' riggers on memory overload-----trying to keep the fuggin' wheels, the fuggin' wings and every fuggin' thing else from fuggin' falling off them big old Hercy birds! I digress-----so back to your book-----very good, very funny, very entertaining. I don't for one minute pretend to be an authority on the written word, far from it. However, in my humble opinion and for what it's worth, your description of Justin and his "living quarters" is brilliant, it paints a real picture of this mysterious guy, it is seriously good. That does'nt mean to say other chapters are not up to scratch, it's just that particular one reads perfectly! Obviously I enjoyed "Gordons Wedding Weekend" ----- sounds like you and the lads also had a good time. I have a feeling that I know that Gordon chap!. I read somewhere that he was a half decent "keeper". It was kind of you to say so. He did eventually have an "artifical" tendon inserted in his "weak" ankle. The surgeon advised that it would last him 10 years, it's done 40 years----so no complaints there!'

Iain Moody: 'Having read your book from back-to-front, my first conclusion was, how did I miss out on all those fleshly lusts that you so eloquently describe, I must have been pre-occupied with my passion for anything with a pair of wings and I don't mean

'Fairies' of the Electronic persuasion. I had no idea that I had mixed with such a crooked, promiscuous, in-disciplined, retro-bate as yourself - isn't jealousy a terrible attribute?' (*where did you get the RAF crest, Ian? And I thought that was a great last sentence! Ed Mac*)

Iain, me and Derek Moore, Tobruk beach, circa 1968

Krusha Richman-Broadbridge (*In trying to locate Julian I found his daughter Krusha on the net and e mailed her. Julian isn't into modern communication methods – and it all went from there- Ed Mac*)

'Hi Mac - I bought Dad your book as a present. It was really fascinating reading about him in his younger 'cool' days, though in fact, he hasn't changed that much, just less hair! I've just spoken to him about meeting up with you & Ken for a drink, he was definitely up for that. He can make

the Friday night in Emsworth, so let me know which is best for you both and I'll pass the details on Hope all is well with you.'
Krusha x

Roger Burke:
'Have really enjoyed reading the book, what a walk down memory lane. I've passed information around about it and also purchased another one as a present. Keep in touch, we must have the reunion, and thanks for a great book.'
Roger (*Ginge in FTOAS chapter 15 Jo Haynes).*

In the above photo, Roger is far right next to Mark Rowe, anyone know who the other two are?

Steve Cash: *(We stayed with Steve's uncle and aunt in Bermuda (FTOAS chapter 23 'The Bermuda Triangle) for a fantastic week courtesy of HM, plus see Steve's other comments later in the chapter 'Lads New contributions' - Ed Mac)*

'The book was a great read and my son is currently reading it and also thinks it's a hoot!'

Steve and I on the bikes everyone rides in Bermuda

Bob Johnson. 'I came across this book by accident and thought I recognised the author's name from my old RAF days. I hadn't seen 'Mac' since the late sixties and decided to buy the book to see what he had to say about our heady days back in the 'Swinging Sixties', and the fun we all had together at the time. I wasn't disappointed: exactly the opposite – he nailed it, and his memories were spot on!

My memories of his excellent dry sense of humour came across immediately – right from the start Mac dives head-first into the action, describing waking up late, inebriated, where he shouldn't be and about to miss his flight on an important RAF detachment overseas – it sets the scene well for the many adventures he goes on to describe.

The book provides thrills, mostly with comely young ladies we befriended at the time, and spills - Mac was well-known for his ill-fated associations with cars. These tales are regularly interspersed with hilarious stories of service life that will resonate with those fortunate enough to have experienced those magical times, but also richly entertain those not privileged to have been around at that time. Everyone reading the book will receive an incredible and amusing insight into what was really happening during the late sixties and early seventies On Her Majesty's Service, within the specialised world of the RAF.

Mac's artistry vividly paints the pictures of the amazing characters he worked with and he describes well the amazing camaraderie so reminiscent of service life. He also describes frankly the good, the bad and the cosmetically-challenged female fraternity we encountered in nurses' homes, teachers' training colleges, telephone exchanges and holiday camps, regularly trawled at that time by a number of us.

In summary I have lent this book to a number of friends and without exception they all considered it to be a brilliantly entertaining read. I have also been asked if I have anymore like it - so I'm just waiting for the sequel to reach the shelves!'

Pat Kerry 'Regarding your book, it sits between the  complete words of Shakespeare and Aristotle, but yours is the only one read from cover to cover. How could I possibly refuse permission to the only chap ever to introduce the subject of piles in possibly our 1st conversation together. It was on a towing team, sitting on a chock by the back door and you warned me of the haemeroidal dangers of attaching the chock to my backside! Subsequent conversations improved.......

I well remember Robbie Robins the plod, you and he organised a football match against the Pongos one Sunday morning. You couldn't find anyone else to referee it and persuaded me to do it. God what a farce it was, I had a huge crepe bandage on the remains of the wrecked knee and couldn't even keep up with the game. Then you and Robbie decided that 90 minutes was too short by which time I was dying away, and ended up having an argument with you over a disallowed goal at one end while the Pongos were scoring via the side netting at the other. Last time I ever went onto a football pitch. Found out 20 yrs later I had knackered jolly old anterior cruciate jobby.

I envy the idea of you poodling around on a scooter in a nice climate..... hope you get the chance to behave badly again! Damien likes to remind me of my running into the back of the Thorney school head mistress's car with my Lambretta. had just picked up new brake linings in the shop in Emsworth and chased after a grotty Hillman Imp:. Round the bend and the Imp had come to a halt at some roadworks and my brakes were in my pocket........cost me a weeks wages then she wrote to the C.O. cos I hadn't paid for the damage ... fortunately Ian Moody was on hand to help out.

Ex-RAF personnel (*but not known by me previously*)

Jim Parker: Larges......should be spelled Lajes. Pop rivet not pock rivet. Excellent book, RAF humour bang on!

From a professional book critic: Danny Collins, RTN

'My wife opened the mail while I was in the shower and told me there was something for me. 'A book,' she called through the door, 'for review I assume.' 'What's the title?' I shouted back through a mouthful of New Listerine mouthwash. Bloody hell, that stuff tastes good; should be served with a cherry in it.

'Fairy Tales of a Sack,' she said doubtfully, 'except they've left the K off.' Oh Gawd, I thought, a drag queen has sent me her bio. Well, it had to happen sometime. But no, when I finally dressed and looked at the package, the book was called Fairy Tales of an SAC, or Senior Aircraftsman, and subtitled 'A young airman's experiences in the Royal Air Force 1967-72'.

The book runs to 38 comedic episodes in the service life of SAC John McGregor – a local writer who now lives in San Fulgencio. So where were the fairies? Ah, John, or Mac as he was known in the service, was an aircraft radio mechanic, known as fairies to differentiate them from the 'heavies' who worked in engines and airframes. Whew, that's got that out of the way... You don't want to upset these RAF lads, even the fairies. I once pronounced it 'raf' in front of an old expat here on the Costa and the old boy went apoplectic. It's AR –AY –EF, see?

The point here is that John McGregor has a delightfully dry wit that had me chuckling out loud – baleful looks from my wife, who thought I was reading about drag queens. It's not a book for cover to cover reading in one sitting, these sort of books never are, but rather to pick up when you've got a few minutes to put your feet up and be amused. It's a little pricey at €16 – that's sterling converted to euros plus P&P - and here I'll have my usual gripe about book publishing in general. Professional writers work on commissions and are paid for what they do. Unknown writers don't and have to recoup the price columns like this to spread the word.

John McGregor has written a fine book and deserves a few punters, so buy the book – just straighten your wife out about the title first, okay?'

Various ladies

Diane *(a fellow student on the same Open University course I studied, who bought a copy)*:

'I finished your book! I love your style of writing, it seems so relaxed and fluid - like you've been writing for years! Very funny too, well done! Do I think it's more for male readers...? Yes, I think I do. I think from a woman's point of view it would have been nice to have been less about the ladies and more about the scrapes you and the guys got into regarding the actual air force. Like the catering escapade, or the cracked wing and the extra-long stay in Bermuda.

I loved all the detail about the forces never having experienced it myself of course and the nostalgia for a bygone era! But no, nothing offended me - too much truly shocking stuff 'out there' nowadays. 54 copies sold in three days in Waterstones is brilliant! I plugged it on my forum a couple of weeks ago so I hope that boosted your Amazon sales!! ;o)) So, when are you starting on a novel...? Diane xx'

Maureen *(a lady reader in the local Writing Circle in Spain I attend):* 'Before reading this book I passed it on to a friend of mine who joined the RAF at the same time as John. Geoff thoroughly enjoyed the book, and being reminded of those days – the escapades of rampant young airmen and the camaraderie that accompanied their work and exploits. So when he returned it to me I was already looking forward to an entertaining read, and hoped to gain some insight into what my Dad, a bomber pilot during WW2, really got up to whilst proclaiming his innocence of all the sins that servicemen are said to indulge in.

I was, of course, expecting it to be a 'man's book', not really of interest to women, but John's talent for dry wit and wry commentary won me over straight away. He is a born storyteller (which is probably why he got away with so much in his younger days!).

It's written as if John is in the room talking to you and reveals as much about the man he is now, as it does about his youthful activities and aspirations. It also confirms that when men get together 'on the pull' there is no way a woman has a hope of preserving her dignity – in their eyes she'll fall into one of their pre-designated categories come what may.

Life in the RAF was clearly a great deal of fun with several hardships to be endured as befitted honourable servicemen. After reading 'Fairy Tales of a SAC' I would say that the latter description did not always strictly apply – thank goodness! A great read, very funny, thanks John. Maureen.'

Linda - *a certain lady who was in the book,*

'Hi Mac! Hardy (she of the broad beam!) here, aka Paula in your book, which I heard about through my brother who recognised the article and picture of you in the Portsmouth Evening News.

I now have a copy of your book and have just started reading it - I loved the Laurel & Hardy chapter, recognising myself, Jill & Steve! I contacted Jill yesterday & gave her the details of your book, another sale I think, I also gave her your e-mail address. Her flabber has never been so gasted when I told her about Laurel & Hardy, and we had a great time reminiscing. It brought back so many memories of the great times we had with you lot over on 'Horney' Island & here on Hayling, they were really fun & carefree days. I hope you don't mind me contacting you, good luck with your book, it evokes such wonderful memories.

PS – finished the book now & thoroughly enjoyed it! Cheers, Hardy! (Real name Linda...)'

(Ed John note – Thanks, Linda – I loved the 'Horney Island' bit...)

An older lady whom I hardly knew *(This lady bought a copy, and came up to me about a week later with this fantastic comment):*

'Oh John, about your book - I'm reading something really heavy at the moment... (*I thought she was going to say that she hadn't had time to read mine*) ... and so I keep your book by my bed, and read a chapter every night before I go to sleep. I have a good old laugh and it sends me off to sleep in a great mood'. (*Well, if I've made one old lady happy, then that can't be bad...*)

And lastly, my 'little' brother - all of six feet two, but seven years younger.

'OK bro....here are my 'considered' comments about your first book (hopefully the first of many)

- It gripped me - I read it all within 3 days. Very readable & fast moving and I continuously wanted to know 'the next bit'
- I liked the notion of lots of individual episodes - all about the same character...you
- I think (but could be wrong) that it will appeal more to blokes than to women (explicit)
- I like the little 'quips' throughout, i.e. " I wonder where she is now" or '"Boom bang a bang" etc
- Like the fact that the times are famous i.e. the Swinging Sixties, but that the book is in a parallel part of that timescale - an alternative version going on in the RAF

- I like it's 'earthiness', i.e. you express what a lot of blokes strive for - sex, booze and a good time and make no pretence of other aspirations
- The humour is you - comes over a lot - and you don't take yourself too seriously
- Like the descriptions of people - the way you paint them
- Interesting use of timescales going backwards and forwards but generally heading through your 5 years RAF life
- It creates the character - YOU! Ready for the next book.

The other element (for me) were the insights of my older brother i.e. I got to better know what you did & experienced at a time when you'd left home and up until this time I was completely unaware of e.g. your feelings when Mum was in Mapperly, your relationship with Dad improving during that period etc. That was really good.

Hope the sales of it are going well. I hope other tomes are underway i.e. Confessions of a Nicholas Salesman, The Later Years, Life on a Spanish Costa etc plus the novels etc.

I'm proud of you BB. You planned it, wrote it, published it and that takes real dedication and talent.

    Keep it going, Allan

4. FIFTEEN MINUTES OF FAME

Book Signing

meet **John McGregor**

author of **Fairy Tales of an SAC**

A young airman's experiences at RAF Thorney Island (and other exotic places) 1967-72

"...a nostalgic treat for anyone who served in the RAF or who recalls the South Coast during those years."

in this store 10am–3pm
WEDNESDAY 16ᵗʰ NOVEMBER 2011

ISBN 1-84683-109-1 | softback | 180 pages | £9.95

In the publishing world they call it 'Public Relations', or 'marketing' don'cha know. It was Andy Warhol who said everyone is supposed to have fifteen minutes of fame at some time in their lives. I think I had mine when FTOAS first came out, after I had put a great deal of personal effort behind getting the word round. Tip: unless you're J.K. Rowling don't expect your publisher, or anyone else for that matter to do the publicity for you - most of it is a DIY job. So in 2010 I had the book published, at last, for me almost a lifetime's work. Now - how will I get it sold? By whom? To whom? Hmm... Well, I reasoned: I've been in sales for most of my working life – so how about it, John? Get selling...

With Hampshire and West Sussex particularly in mind as my target area, early in 2011 I came over to the UK from Spain where I live, and, stayed with Martin in Southsea. My great mate of over 40 years (that's duration, not his age) was then still working hard to solve serious crime as a dedicated senior policeman in Hampshire. Like the good friend he is helped me out manfully where he could, like driving me to interviews or loaning me his Satnav a couple of times to find places I needed to. We still always had a laugh together while doing it, as we have continued to do over the years we have known each other. I think he enjoyed the change, especially when we listened to the radio interview where the poor woman couldn't shut me up!

I decided the booksellers Waterstones were the key to selling success: they are the only national chain of pure booksellers that are dedicated to the job. Not only did they sell books, they had branches in all the right places, so they were my key routes to success. I rang up the branch managers of the stores in Chichester, Portsmouth and their two shops in Southampton, and made appointments to see them all. To a man, or woman the staff at Waterstones were extremely helpful, I couldn't fault them. It transpired that in each shop they had 'Events Managers' who were responsible for promotions and demonstrations - such as book signings – which is where I wanted to be.

As the book was already published I had the necessary ISBN code number, the first thing Waterstones asked for. I presented my book to every member of the staff I could, and explained of the potential local interest it would generate, aided by the fact that many ex-Thorney RAF people still lived in the area of those two counties. Every branch agreed to help me, and they would each book an 'Event' and order in 20 copies per branch via their own distribution system, through their central warehouse called 'The Hub'. The lead times involved meant that it needed several weeks to get from branch order placed to the Hub, then back to my publisher in Bognor for initial delivery. I still had a great deal to learn about the publishing world, but my career experience in sales helped a great deal. Wow, 80 books (gulp) - hope I can pull it off...

The book signing events were agreed for consecutive days during the second week in September 2011: Thursday 11th in Chichester near The Cross, Friday 12th in Portsmouth's Commercial Road Shopping Centre, and on 13th Saturday morning in the smaller Southampton High Street store and the afternoon in Waterstones pin-up store in the West Quay Shopping Centre of the city. My publisher produced window and instore bills as per the picture for each branch and these were sent directly to the stores.

However, to support these events I needed more help if the operation was to be successful. I went to see the Portsmouth Evening News and the Southampton Echo and was interviewed by their reporters, both of whom again were extremely helpful. They took notes and I provided them with relevant pictures to go with the articles. With the weekly Chichester Observer and its several other West Sussex publications I used the phone and e mail to liaise with a very helpful journalist called Phil Hewitt to get the necessary information to him for his newspaper articles. All the press played their part and generously gave me excellent articles on the book, complete with old and new photos from those days with explanatory write ups: I treasure these cuttings, as they opened up many doors as detailed elsewhere.

The final supporting part was via the wonderful media of radio – local radio. Again by the telephone and e mail I contacted BBC Radio Solent and was given a 10 minute spot on Katie Martin's afternoon show a few days before the book signings. There I was able to tell people about Fairy Tales, what it was all about, how they could buy a copy and our forthcoming plans for a full reunion. It worked wonderfully as a number of ex-Thorney people heard the interview and came to the book signings, others contacted me by e mail or phone as per the details supplied in the press and in the interview.

Waterstones were as good and efficient as they had promised. On arrival for the first book signing in Chichester, duly bearing the window bills instore and outside, several yards inside the lovely old listed building near the Cross was a table covered by a black cloth, a chair and a pile of twenty books. I had also bought some Hercules pin badges from the RAFA and used these as give-aways with each purchase. Derek Heard, an old RAF friend whose name appears elsewhere in this book had been in and left me a copy of the previous week's local paper. I hadn't yet seen it, and the paper contained a wonderful article by the said Phil Hewitt, with all the relevant details of the book signing. Quite simply I could not have asked for more support and a better start. Ooh-er, my bluff was well and truly called. Now all I had to do was sell some books…

That first morning at Chichester was amazing, which I won't forget in a hurry. It was indeed the start of my 15 minutes of fame. From eleven o'clock start until lunchtime I had a steady stream of 'old' friends who had got the message via the P/R and duly came in to meet me and buy a signed book. I have already written about the riveting surprise I got from my old flame Jill, but also came Paddy MacGill, Pete and Brenda Cox and Peter Middlebrook and his wife. This initial burst, however, couldn't last and after lunchtime things quietened down a little. I had done well, I thought, having sold and signed eight books - but I soon began to realise it wouldn't always be like this – and I still had twelve books left to sell. I quickly learned that the art of selling your own books is not to sit around waiting for people to come up, and say things like:

'Ooh, this looks interesting – tell me about it' - because it just won't happen, believe me. The secret is to be pro-active, and look for sales yourself. After all, I thought - what are people in Waterstones shops there doing? They have come in because they are interested in books – and you've got one to sell. No-one knows your product better then you, so just like selling anything in life, you stress its good points – and go for it. Book in hand I prowled round the store and approached people during the afternoon, and told 'em about it.

The lovely Denise, the Waterstones girl in charge of Events kept me well supplied and lubricated with coffees and teas – and I persevered. By four o'clock I had sold seven more copies to all sorts of different people, total fifteen for the day, and was complimented by the Waterstones staff, who were quietly watching. They told me they had had authors in who had sold none, or only one or two copies all day. The manager, Matt and his staff were quite happy to keep the five left in stock for customers who hadn't been able to get to the store on the day. What a baptism of fire: I loved it...

The next day in Portsmouth was different: no early birds this time but I did get visits and purchases from my old friend Ken Patchett, who apart from his waistline hadn't changed a bit, and one or two other 'old' mates I hadn't seen for years. I was in Commercial Road Shopping Centre, strangely enough just up the road from our old stamping ground, the Mecca with all its memories, the building now long since gone. I needed to attack sales early, and then keep up the pace all day. I felt by now I was sharpening my sales approach and getting better all the time. Through the

Writing Circle I had joined in Spain I met a published author called Penny Legg, who had given me some valuable advice about publishing and book signings. Penny lives in Hampshire, and she turned up in the afternoon with her husband and we chatted happily for a while.

There was also one lovely experience in the afternoon with a certain lady written which I've about elsewhere in this book, see the 'Twinkle in your Eye' chapter 12 story. By four o'clock, tired-but-happy I had done one better than Chichester: sixteen sold and signed, only four left that they kept. Thanks Pompey, great memories!

Saturday 13th September, 2011 – what a day... Unlike Chichester and Portsmouth I was unfamiliar with downtown Southampton, I only recall the old Dell for Southampton football and the Top Rank Dance Hall, both now since sadly gone. The High Street Waterstones store was the smallest of the four, rather confusingly on two floors and used by many people as a cut through from the car park behind the main shopping area - but for three hours from ten until one o'clock I worked hard – and sold and signed eight books. The young manager there was concerned about having 12 copies left, so we settled for him keeping two and liaising with the very co-operative and efficient West Quay staff I took ten with me to their flagship store, just inside the front door of the giant Shopping Centre. Now then, John, a new and final challenge – not 20 to sell – 30!

West Quay Waterstones has everything going for it: terrific staff, a welcoming atmosphere, an instore cafe - Chi and Portsmouth have one too, but not so much a part of the store as Southampton's refreshment area with a big Costa Coffee Shop, it's a very sociable place. Because shoppers have to pass the bookshop's huge front doors on their way into the West Quay Centre the traffic is good - and I had a key spot just inside the big doors. Game on! I never stopped for the next four hours, I didn't sit down once. It's a good job I can talk 'til the cows come home – it came in handy that day. An ex-RAF boffin bought a copy, and then kindly got hold of my smartphone, downloading the RAF March music onto it as a ringtone alert – that was very kind, and funny, but I had to knock it off as it was driving me mad!

By five o'clock I had sold and signed twenty-six books at West Quay alone, surprising both the store management – and me! The Events manageress who I had met previously was off work sick for a few days, but the lovely assistant manager Sue and I got on famously, see picture.

So in three wonderful days I had sold and signed sixty-five books – and I'm very proud of that, considering I am no natural author and hadn't done anything like that before. Never, ever in my wildest dreams had I thought that at 62 I would be actively walking round bookstores selling something very precious to me. If I never write anything else I will always be proud of Fairy Tales, and where the book has taken me. With those precious three days and the excellent radio interview on BBC Radio Solent I think I truly had my fifteen minutes of fame. Not only was it such new fun, it helped to put me back in touch with many 'old' friends I had long since forgotten and/or lost touch with - and who I never thought I would see again. Happy days!

5. 242 OCU

Diplomats, acrobats, comedians, performers, barrack-room lawyers, smart-asses, smelly asses, farters, artists, con artists, piss-artists (we had a few of them), sportsmen, raconteurs, good eggs, bad eggs, rotten eggs, halitosis sufferers, bigguns, smalluns, blackuns, brownuns, whiteuns, bullshitters, flashers, card sharps, Bridge experts, dart aces, hypercondriacs, quacks, medical experts – and many more types of airmen I met in the magical crewroom of 242 OCU in 1968, the 'college' I found in a strange wooden 'H' block, up on the airfield of 'Hercules First Line' at Thorney. This room's inhabitants shaped my personality for ever, over a wonderful four-year period of my life from

1968 to 1971 inclusive: I was aged eighteen, and a little naive when I first walked in, and coming up twenty-three when I left: what an education in life that room gave me...

The next paragraph names names of those I remember from Herc 1st – or should that be 'Erk' First? -at the time, and those who now delightfully attend the reunions. I am refusing to link any of them to the types of character I described earlier, that I met in the infamous crewroom: that's my story and I'm sticking to it. You knew who/what you are/were, so if the beret fits... In no particular order, the roll call is:

Ron Eldridge, Ken Patchett, Julian Richman-Broadbridge, John 'Flash' Burton, Paddy Hagan, Les Prior, Al (Damian) Thomas, Roger (Ging) Burke, Syd Thorpe, Errol (Mac) MacBean, Russ Brockbank, John Drew, Pat Kerry, Ed Spencer, Glyn Childs, Martin Shuker, Pete Cox, Pete Stevens, Pete Freeman, Pete Middlebrook, Steve Cash, Mark Rowe, Glenn Parker, Bob Heyhoe, Geoff Hobbs, Clive Hall, Graham Newman, John Emburton, Chris Bell & Chalkie Richardson. If I've missed you out and you feel aggrieved let me know and I'll amend the list.

My over-riding memory of 242 OCU is one of laughter. You could never get a swelled head in the crew-room, there was always someone to cut you down to size: sarcasm and piss-taking was the order of the day, and we had past-masters at it. Quiet it wasn't and if the atmosphere dulled there was always sparks like Paddy Hunter to liven it up. He would make outrageous statements, like:

'Oi cannot drive safely on de English roads without at least four pints inside me,' to which someone would retort:

'That's bollocks Paddy!', but then someone else would chip in and say:

'No, I agree, I know what he means, that goes for me too', and in no time a full-blown argument would be going on. Paddy would then sit back proudly and listen, his job done to perfection.

'If dere's one ting oi can't stand', he'd say 'Its a quiet crew room!'

Hercules Handling Flight
Royal Air Force, Thorney Island

Summer Social

at the
"Thatched House", Locksway Road, Milton.

on

Wednesday June the 4th. 1969

commencing at 8 p.m.

Dress Optional. (Admit One)

One of the many 'Herc 1st' Social Do's

We would sometimes go on detachment, but if the walls and the temperature varied, the humour did not and the memories are still vivid: Libya (El Adem, shudder, see chapter 9 of FTOAS), Malta (the Gut), Cyprus (fantastic, except for Kokkinelli...). Here's a story, one which i still remember, which sort of sums up the quirky education I was given free by my elder tutors. One lunchtime in white-hot El Adem an older, married bloke I vaguely knew and I were on duty together while everyone else was at lunch. He turned to me and said solemnly:

'You're a young, single lad, I'm going to tell you a story. Once upon a time there was a young lad, bit like yourself. He'd had one or two girlfriends, but nothing special. Then one dark night he met this girl. He was stunned, he thought she was so beautiful. The girl was very quiet, he put it down to shyness, but she let him take her home, and they started to go out together. He couldn't believe his luck, she was so lovely, although she said very little. He just thought when she knew him better she'd open up.

Eventually he met her parents, and soon, as he was so smitten he asked her to marry him. She said yes, although little else but he assumed she would naturally talk more when they got married. They did get married, however she still didn't say a lot. He presumed if and when they had children, she would talk more. Well, they did – have children - and she didn't. One day, after ten years of marriage and two lovely children it suddenly hit him, very hard between the eyes – just why she never said anything.'

My older colleague stopped talking and stared at me. Everything went quiet, even the mozzies.

'Why didn't she say anything-?' I asked, baffled.

'Because she'd got fugg-all to say!' He shouted back, almost triumphantly. I learnt a lot that day: another lesson in my education at the knee of the old lags - no disrespect to anyone intended. It sort of tied in something my late lovely Mum used to say: 'some people sits and thinks – others just sit'. I was only 18 when I hit the crewroom running, and just about everybody was older than me. Strangely enough, at the reunions they still are...

One of the senior citizens was called Colin Urry, and he had that rare ability to be able to sketch it how it was, to capture true 242 OCU life. One of his efforts was stuck on the crew-room wall, it was a 'snapshot' of the hold of a Hercules somewhere over the Alps. The picture aptly depicted vibration, it always seemed to me every nut and bolt shook when the gigantic Herc engines were running. All around the huge cargo bay airmen were sitting, vertical, horizontal, sitting, lounging, sleeping, eating, drinking coffee, farting, belching etc as men do when they are together (well, make that anytime). The scene depicted was a kind of temporary mad hell, the highly uncomfortable passage of men in a big metal cell high in the air hurtling from one place to another, a temporary five to six hours of being shaken about till you were numb everywhere, deafened by the experience, the kites (planes) serviced by the boozy buggers you were out drinking with the previous nights. The caption under the perfect picture read:

'It must be great on the Hercs – you're always off somewhere exciting!'. To that I would say it was always 'great' when we got there – El Adem excepted. It didn't do to have a bad hangover, an upset stomach or similar affliction when travelling on a Herc for any length of time. I experienced a few 'Navexes', flying across oceans with journeys of 12 – 14 hours at a time in those wonderful marvels made by Lockheed – and do you know what? I wouldn't have missed a second of it. I can feel and experience it now, the vibration and noise. My mates, the old riggers might have something to say (see Graham Logg's comments in chapter three 'Original Book Comments' but for me I loved those aircraft, and still get a buzz when i see them on the news or in a TV program – or even a rare one flying overhead. There was even a Herc I spotted sitting way out at Alicante airport last year, no idea what it was doing there.

Back to 242 OCU: it really is funny, nut humorously funny, but experience-in-life funny when I see those 'old' faces now at the reunions, these days nearly fifty years since I first met them in the line hut on the airfield. Weathered with the passage of time, yes, but still the same humour is there when we meet that I'll always remember, the free education in life I received courtesy of Her Majesty. Those four years 'Up The Line' were probably the happiest of my life in some ways, when I was young, free and single – and met some of the greatest characters in life I could possibly have – thanks, lads!

6. FAIRY TALES OF AN SAC

When you write a book, one that's about people who've been in your life a long time ago, you never, ever think you're going to meet those people again – or in my case I never dreamed I would. But that, of course is exactly what happened to me, in spades, with 'Fairy Tales Of An SAC', or FTOAS as the publisher calls it. I left the RAF in 1972, and, agreed, it took me thirty-seven years until 2009 to write the book, but when I did the words flowed out reasonable easily: I really didn't have to think too hard. After all, I had carried all the stories around in my head for those long years, recounted mainly to myself, but also to friends, family and anyone else who'd listen. To me the stories and the people never changed or aged, they were just as fresh to me when I wrote them down as if they had just happened. What's that classic 'Ozzy Osborne' line? 'I can remember what happened thirty years ago like it was yesterday. The fookin' trouble is, I can't remember what did happen yesterday!'. Bang on Ozzy...

For the book I treated each story I remembered as a separate chapter, and soon I had thirty-eight tales running across individual persons, actual events and comments on various periods and attitudes I experienced in my own 'little' RAF career. I am well aware that my six months of training, plus four and a half years at the wonderful Thorney Island do not qualify me to be an authority on the RAF, the forces or anything military, indeed most of those I met and feature here all did much longer service. I prefer my FTOAS to be read and seen as a snapshot of a certain life in the RAF on the south coast in the late sixties and early seventies – through my eyes only...I know I was very lucky to spend virtually all my service days on a camp like Thorney, where we were left to our own devices up on the airfield, and such other emotive forces issues like the length of your hair and the state of your uniform were not the main point of you being there: the aircraft, in our case the wonderful Hercules were king. 'First Line' meant keeping them up there fully serviced at all times and we did...

People have remarked on the slightly curious time scale running through FTOAS. Although I could have put the chapters into a reasonably accurate, logical time frame, initially I sent my 'masterpiece' as it was to several people I knew to appraise, and two or three actually advised me to leave it as it was. That meant starting on a lively note with a story from the middle of my service time that demonstrates a lot of the content, and finishing the book with a final story about leaving the RAF - and in between not overly worrying too much about the sequential time aspect. Hence the rude awakening to start, opening my eyes to find I was somewhere I shouldn't have been with a serious hangover, and late for flying off on an important overseas detachment – but somehow scraping through, as ever. I was dead lucky in all my five years, I bent the rules a few times, but always got away with it. I am a lucky man in many ways in my life, and those five years got me off to a flyer (RAF joke…).

While studying writing techniques on the Open University 'Creative Writing' course I did about five years ago, I came across some advice called the 'RUE' aspect. That stands for 'Resist the Urge to Explain', so in my case, just because certain aspects didn't follow a logical or expected pattern, let the reader worry about it and work it out, not you – so that is what I did. It seemed to work for FTOAS, as hardly anyone ever mentioned it. I've done a few talks on the book to various organizations here in Spain and sold some signed copies afterwards, and I also try to sum up the stories using alliteration, another writing skill I picked up along the way during the wonderful OU course, which was excellent. Lads, lasses, life, love, laughter… they all sum up FTOAS up nicely.

It is very nice and encouraging to have now sold well over 1,500 copies of a niche-type book about forces life from almost 50 years ago, but the best part for me, by far has been the journey Fairy Tales has taken me on – and one that is still progressing, bless… Of course, I wrote the book initially for myself, as I had always wanted to get it all down on paper, and hoped I could in a sort-of logical, humorous way. But secretly I hoped some of the 'old' gang I spent those fantastic five years with would get to read it, like it and it would bring them back memories, and take them all the way back to those great days. Of course, there was also my wonderful family who lovingly supported me, as ever in my life, and enthused that support with great comments. Example:

'Can I play you in the film?' my brother asked.

'No, of course not', I told him. 'You're much too old and fat (he's not – fat that is, the skinny get). I told him 'Your son might be able to, although of course he isn't as good-looking as I was..'. You have to stand up for yourself in a big family, and give as good as you get. We still all meet up for a week's holiday every year, and the banter flies around mercilessly…

Well, the 'old' RAF lads steadily got copies, read FTOAS and – well, modesty forbids me. No it doesn't John, read chapter three - but those comments really did mean so much to me as they steadily came in. Some even gave me the compliment that their sons had read it, and exactly similar to my own son marvelled at the things we got up to, each father and colleague with his own unwritten stories and personal memories from those fabulous days – when all we were really doing was 'serving our Queen and Country' as a certain character in the book observed (Ron Eldridge). If I have to define the audience FTOAS was primarily aimed at, it would be my old mates from 242 OCU, my friends that I shared the fun and frolics from that period in my life with, that I will never forget.

The even better bit then began when we started

to get back in touch with each other, all because of the book and the prospect of us all meeting up formally as a real reunion began to slowly become a reality. When eventually, at last we all met up on 'The Glorious Twelfth', i.e. Saturday 12th May 2012, it was an occasion I will never forget. Nearly 100 old friends coming together in The Sailing Club at Thorney, quite simply the most perfect place it could possibly be, the scene of so many memories. Unbelievably, like most of Thorney the place remains unchanged - how refreshing in these rapidly-changing days. One wit, who shall remain nameless quipped:

'I burst into the bar of the Sailing Club, expecting to see those slim, virile young men I had served with years ago. Inside were a load of fat old men with drinks in their hands, all red-faced and laughing...'. I thought that was a great summary of the first reunion, albeit a tad harsh? (if the beret fits, wear it, John). Yes, agreed, the lads were all older, some plumper, some without a lot of hair, some greyer, whiter, thinner, but yes – it was 'them' - those lads who had formed that very impressionable part of my life way back then, the ones I had written about and who I had never forgotten over that long period of time. We were now all 're-united' with our stories to remind us of those great days, and tell each other of how we'd been in the interim years - and adding to the database with new/old recollections. Like last year I was told:

'When you went out on the razz you used to carry a toothbrush round, poking out of your top suit pocket, as a conversation piece in case you pulled, you used it as a chat-up line'. When I tried to deny it (I have honestly completely forgotten I did that) other 'witnesses' were called, who confirmed it. So I suppose I must have done – wonder if it worked?

'The Magnificent Seven'.

This picture of the first reunion appeared in the Chichester Observer in 2013. From left to right: Syd Thorpe, Martin, Mac, Ron Eldridge, Steve Cash, Nick Pomfret and Roger Burke

In summary, this follow-up one is a book about life, about what has happened since writing FTOAS. In it I hope to bring back to life what happened forty-odd years ago, what has happened to us all since, and how we now all meet up again and have a great laugh about those wonderful days. Since FTOAS came out I have since written another book, and am in the middle of another. They are both 'life' stories, which is what I do, write about life. I find it much more interesting and exciting than any fiction. But in terms of where FTOAS has taken me, which means so much that there can never be anything that will ever come up to the original Fairy Tales, or anywhere near. If you have read this book, then thanks, and please, as ever let me know any feedback: it is much appreciated!

7. MARTIN SHUKER

Corporal Shuker and his beloved Wolsey (look at those sideboards!)

I woke up early in the morning with a thick head – no change there... I was lying on my back in a strange bed in a strange room, but the most worrying factor was that I was not alone. There was a man lying next to me, facing my side. He was big, fair-headed with a large, beaky nose and a stubbly chin, He was too close for comfort, so I elbowed him, and he opened one eye.

'Hey Mac' he said conversationally. 'I never

told you I was queer, did I?' We didn't use the word 'gay' in those days, but despite all the overwhelming evidence to the contrary I had seen from him up to that particular morning, just for one horror-struck moment he had me fooled. The petrified look on my face cracked him up, and he burst out laughing in a maniacal cackle and thankfully moved away. This incident summed up Martin William Shuker's sense of humour perfectly: my great friend was always up for a piss-take, as were most servicemen you came across while serving her Majesty: it was second nature.

Just to explain - we had gone to Jersey for a fortnight's holiday. Robbie, the only RAF Policemen we liked, and who was one of our gang came from the main Channel island, and told us we could stay with his widower dad while there, if we liked. Being hard-up servicemen we agreed like a shot. Robbie told us his dad was 'a bit of a cranky old boy' – and he was! Little did we know we had to share a double bed, the first and last time I ever did so in my life – once was enough. I knew from then on what women have to put with, their men snoring and farting away all night...

In FTOAS I introduced my best mate as 'Steve'. The code was 'Steve Martin' – i.e. Martin. Martin Shuker, to be precise is my best friend in life. We have known each other about 47 years now which is a long time, and I always say we have been good mates through all life's trials and tribulations – and we've both had a few of them. At the time of writing I'm one marriage up on him, but he might be equalizing sometime. You never know...

I don't think we were instantly friends. I always accused him of snobbery at first as initially when he came to Thorney in 1968 he tended to knock around some lads he had known in Germany while posted there, and he seemed a bit aloof in those days. Always senior to me, a mere SAC, Mart was first a J/T, and soon became a corporal. As an NCO he was soon in charge of various jobs and teams of people, and as such carried more authority - which unlike certain others never changed him. But now having responsibilities and recognised as a leader he often roped me, a mere Fairy and a few others to rally round and help out - which when on 'Nights' was a good move, so that we can all finish early - a powerful weapon in those heady days of singlies partying whenever we could.

Martin became the big brother in life I had never had. About 18 months older, he had joined the RAF as a boy entrant at 15, whereas mine was 'Direct Entry'. I was just under 18 when I joined in 1967. He was also that most hard-working and put-upon of aircraft trades, airframes, or a rigger as they are known colloquially. Me being a 'Fairy', aka an aircraft radio mechanic don'cha know our friendship was perhaps unlikely. But we gradually got to know each other better and eventually started to knock about together, firstly in a group but eventually joining up to hunt as a pair. That enabled making previously-agreed rules, unspoken in public - like taking it in turns to go for the 'best' one when out on the razz, a much-debated subject later which usually ended in many post-mortems, often in the mess the day after with much ribald comment and joking.

The holiday was great, the biggest of the Channel Islands, Jersey was/is a fantastic place. One of the games we played there was to tell young ladies we were professional footballers on holiday, and in the dark – very dark – we could just about pass for two Portsmouth footballers of the day, David Munks (Martin) and Brian Bromley (me). In reality and in the daylight we looked more like Bobby Ball and Tommy Cannon! I suppose in these very PC days we could get done for impersonating well-known people (now that would have been funny, given Martin's career), but in those carefree days nobody much cared. I remember drinks were expensive in Jersey, so we would go down the local bars early to get a few in – make that a lot in – before attacking the town.

'Footballers' on St Brelades Bay beach in Jersey

Actually, football 'kicked in' in a big way with us, both watching Portsmouth (dire) and Southampton (brilliant) on alternative weekends, and playing, first for the station, then later for a civvy team called Eastoke on nearby Hayling Island. Martin was always a better footballer than me, much more experienced, but big-brother style always encouraged me on the field, sometimes in a not-too-friendly manner: 'Get stuck into him, Mac; harder, he likes it!' he would bellow. As it happened, I needed little encouragement that way, as what I lacked in skill I easily made up for in 'enthusiasm', which is a nice way to say I got stuck in. Mind you, I saw 'Shooks' sent off one day against one of our perennial opponents, the Navy when he came up against a mirror copy of himself in midfield. They were both sent off for kicking each other, and more after only 20 minutes: tee hee!

In those halcyon days my big brother protected me at certain key times: like when I was daft with money (often), stopping me stupidly buying rounds when it wasn't my turn, and telling me off severely when I loaned my newish girlfriend £30 – which was a lot of money in those days. There's a lot more to that story (I married her, but we'll leave that for another day...). Mart also came to help me one dark night when three blokes set on me in Southsea. Three (!) of us were walking down a dark road on our way to an Indian restaurant after a night on the beer - and three young ladies were coming the other way.

The numbers seemed convenient, so I asked them where they were going, not realising they were walking just ahead of their boyfriends. The three women weren't exactly out of the top drawer of life, and I was given a colourful mouthful of abuse in reply. I'm not sure whether I had a chance to say anything else, I may have said something like 'Charming!' but the next second something hit me hard in the face and I heard a belligerent voice claim 'That's my missus!', and I went down under a hail of blows. Our third 'friend', who shall remain nameless bravely ran off, but my true mate came to help me and got thumped himself for his trouble. I seem to remember being more miffed about my new lambswool pullover, now-ripped with bloodstains all down the front than any physical discomfort. Cheers though, Mart,- what a mate...

It wasn't all one way though, no sir. Conversely, I always say I cleaned up more of his puke (sorry, but its true) than any woman 'Shuker-the-Puker' was ever involved with. Of course, that is a perfectly natural response to over-indulging in alcohol, which for some reason he did, but I never had the luxury –or otherwise – of. So we looked out for each other, as good mates do... Martin was my best man when I married the nurse (the £30 one!), and did a good job, as one would expect of a fine upstanding NCO in Her Majesty's Service.

Martin lasted longer than I did in the RAF after I left in 1972. He married Liz and they moved to East Anglia, but we stayed in contact over many house moves. The RAF's loss was the Hampshire Police's gain, and Martin once again rose through the ranks to become a leader of men, a detective inspector. All I can say from my side is that I'm glad I wasn't ever being interviewed by him, he's so thorough he'd have the truth out of you, no problem. In 1998 I moved to Spain to live, and Martin has come out every year to stay with my wife and i. When I was writing FTOAS it was Mart who reminded me of several incidents to put in, the one we always laugh about was chapter 10. 'Cracking the Mess'. What a laugh that was, we were dead lucky we didn't get caught.

M & M – Mac and Martin 2014

In turn I have spent a number of holidays with my great mate in his house in Southsea, and I always look forward to them as the area always brings me back literally to the scenes of much of the crimes, to keep it topical. 'Poacher turned Gamekeeper' comes to mind, although we never were criminals, we just got away with a lot, and both of us have lived to tell the tale. Now we are both pensioners, but neither of us are gardeners or bowls players, and we do different things which keep us busy, me in Spain and Martin on the south coast.

Lately Martin went to Tangmere, the old Battle of Britain station to see the RAF museum there – and got a job! The bloke showing him round was so impressed with the old rigger's knowledge when they looked over the Lightning and the Harrier at Tangmere, both of which he had previously worked on. They offered him a position there and then, which the hands-on mechanic graciously accepted. Mart says its very like the RAF with the laughs he has with the blokes he works with. He's promised to take me there and show me round next time I'm over, which I'm really looking forward to.

In conclusion of this chapter i would like to pay tribute to a really good friend. I am so glad, and proud we have kept in touch over the years and shared so many experiences in our lives. Although we both have brothers and are from similar families and backgrounds Martin truly is the brother I never had growing up, and we have helped each other through some of life's lively experiences over the years. He is a good man to have as a friend - I've nearly forgiven him about the double bed incident in Jersey - and he's nearly forgiven me for bending the bumper of his Wolsey when he leant me it for the weekend!

8. BRING ON.....THE TWINS!

This photo wasn't actually of Al Thomas's bed in the block, it was taken at his parents' home on the Isle of Wight,: read on...

I'd nearly finished my words of welcome at our first RAF reunion in The Sailing Club in May 2012. To my utter amazement, due to a last-minute rush caused by a BBC Radio Solent interview I did and local press articles, we had 86 old farts – sorry, make that friends - at the do, all in very varying states of health and appearance, as you would expect of men in the 60 to 80 years category (I'm still one of the youngest, just like when I first walked into the crewroom of 242 OCU). With one or two exceptions, most of us are still fine specimens of British manhood and virility today, as of course we were then, still wearing well, waistlines still trim-ish (?) and turned out smartly casual for the event. We looked like dignified older examples of the cream of Britain's fighting forces from the sixties and seventies – well, that's my story and I'm sticking to it!

However, to leave 'em laughing and get the reunion off to a good start, my great mate and fellow-organiser Martin and I couldn't resist a good old RAF-style wind-up and leg-pull. If you've read 'FTOAS' (and if not, why not, get a copy!) you will know all about 'The Twins'. If you don't, just to briefly paint the scene:

It is during the baking hot summer of 1970, in the aforementioned Thorney Island Sailing Club: a picturesque, sunny spot overlooking the shoreline. This is where we used to relax with a drink or seven when off-duty in those days on the almost all-male camp. But a totally unexpected phenomenon occurred one sweaty Saturday lunchtime. As though somehow coming out of the sun, we knew not from where, two identical, stunning 19 year-old female twins tottered in, their appearance causing a minor sensation with the testosterone-laden, lusty, languishing lads.

The two had shoulder-length blonde hair, wide baby-blue eyes and deceivingly-innocent angelic faces. Body-wise they had the lot, in spades – well, curves, really: tight white low-cut bulging tops, skimpy white hot pants (remember them - steady lads!), acres of milky-white thighs and slender legs disappearing into white stilettos.

You could almost hear the sharp intake of breath from round the large bar, matching the thud of stubbly chins hitting the floor. Within seconds 'The Twins' were surrounded, sitting on knees, sipping drinks provided by willing admirers. For the next couple of months they would suddenly appear, as usual from nowhere, normally at some function or minor celebration – we had a lot of those to pass the time – and naturally they became instantly very popular. Lurid stories quickly circulated and were roundly (!) discussed involving the sexual promiscuity and athleticism of The Twins.

They would unexpectedly and wildly get carried away at unpredictable moments with any fortunate airman they happened to be with, or even just fancied at the time, disappearing into the gents, down the shoreline, in backs of cars, wherever was relatively convenient, and not always totally private. They quickly acquired the affectionate nicknames 'Muff and Fluff', although no-one could actually tell which was which. Looking back it seemed to be the uniform that turned them on, they 'performed' better with anyone in serge blue.

If you want to know more specific details of their activities in those days, you'll have the read the chapter 'The Twins' in the book. For the record sadly neither Martin nor I participated directly, quite simply we could never get near 'em! But, and most importantly for this story, a few other close mates did dabble, and these were our main target audience on 'The Glorious Twelfth' - my name for our first reunion on 12th May 2012. As the spoken word about the great day got round, and numbers swelled, often the mock-hilarious question 'Are The Twins/Muff and Fluff coming?' was posed. Now that gave me a wicked idea, which Mart and I couldn't resist. As I wound up my 20 minute introduction I announced, as dead-pan as I could manage:

'Well, ladies and gentleman, before I finish and we can all get on with enjoying the afternoon, Martin and I wanted to bring in two people, without whom a Thorney Island Sailing Club reunion would not be complete'. I paused to look round at vacantly- expectant faces.

'We searched hard - and eventually found them. Up until now we've hidden them in the gents, where of course they spent much of their time during that hot summer of 1970'. Further pause,to look round at amazed faces, spotting ribs being nudged as the message began to sink in. Here we go...

'Martin, will you go and bring in – The Twins!' My big brother got up and purposefully headed for the gents (cue buzz of excited chatter!).

Most people in the room knew who The Twins were - and what they had got up to in those days. There were quite a few of those ex-dabblers present, those lusty lads who had had first-hand and other body experiences, including several who were now with their wives or partners: indeed some attendees had come to the reunion 'accompanied'. Talk about hook, line and sinker – reel 'em in! Martin and I let it run for about thirty seconds before he burst back in, and we pointed at everyone, loudly proclaiming together 'That fooled you!', and everyone roared with laughter – and a few with relief - as we all joined in on the joke.

At the last reunion in 2014 I heard yet another twins' story I hadn't heard before. John Gallagher recounted how he dropped into the infamous Railway Inn early one evening for a pint on his way back to camp. Inside to his surprise he found the twins sitting close beside a surprised young airman in full uniform who had just got off the train. This newbie had just been posted to Thorney and was waiting for the bus. The twins were also going there to attend some function in the Sailing Club they had heard about. Now as mentioned above The Twins' predilection for young men in uniform was well-known (talk to Geordie Woods, or see FTOAS chapter 22 'The Twins') – except to this new young airman, just out of training. John quickly took in the scenario and gallantly (!) offered to take everyone up to the camp in his car.

One twin got in beside him, the other got in the back with the newbie. John chatted to the one beside him on the way up to Thorney, not really noticing the silence in the back. When they arrived at the Sailing Club both twins jumped out and ran into the club laughing between themselves. The young man climbed out, his face a study.

'I don't believe it', he gasped to John. 'She's just tossed me off on the way here!'. Yes, that was just one more of The Twin's escapades and their amazing sexually-charged adventures with our RAF over those summer months in 1970.

For the record, The Twins suddenly disappeared

that summer as quickly as they had come, and no-one was quite sure why or where they'd gone. As we were the only RAF station in that Navy-dominated area near Portsmouth, a rumour abounded that they had transferred their affections to that inferior marine branch of the services - and if so there would have been much work for them to do there! So much, much later, like forty-odd years on during our wonderful similarly-sunny afternoon get-together there was inevitably some speculation and discussion of The Twins – where are they now, we wondered? Still causing mayhem? Or perhaps settled down to domesticity, wild oats very comprehensively sown, now happily married - perhaps, with kids, and maybe grandkids?

Where I live in Sunny Spain there is an expat radio station called Talk Radio Europe (TRE), broadcast from Malaga which is very popular here. Every week they have a book program and the busy presenter, Hannah Murray interviews published authors. I was lucky to be on it with FTOAS but was amazed when the author, or I should say authoress was an American woman called Francine Pascale, She wrote a very famous series of books about teenage life which was made into films, and featured two identical girl twins. Hannah expressed the view that she personally was disappointed reading about them growing up that the twins didn't get into any 'hanky-panky', to which Francine coyly replied that that was the way she liked it, and wanted it to stay.

After that interview it was my turn and I wasn't going to let the 'topical' aspect of their chat pass by. I quickly told Hannah that my book contained a whole chapter about an identical set of twins – and these ones definitely 'did sex'!

'Wow, John!' said Hannah (she was a great sport). 'Was that personal experience, that you're writing about them from?'

'Alas, no, Hannah,; I replied truthfully. 'Quite honestly, I could never get near enough!' -and that's the truth...

OK, folks, we actually have an expert – no, make that a 'sexpert' on The Twins. Come in, our very own Al (Damian) Thomas:

'The Twins? OMG what can I say, I enjoyed every single minute with them. Liz and Caz they were, or when meeting their Mum and Dad, Elizabeth and Catherine. My Dad never got over the time I took them home for the Easter weekend one year.... Damn, that was sooooooo funny. Just before Dad died we were talking and he suddenly burst out laughing as he remembered them and the lengths my Mum took to try and keep us apart while we stayed over - all to no avail I may add!

I would like to put one matter straight before it all goes downhill (even more). The Twins were not responsible for the 'Crabs' episode on Thorney, that was down to 55 Air Dispatch Troop shagging everything in sight, even the local dogs. I remember going on earlies one very cold, frosty morning and all the Pongos were lined up outside their Block, stark naked, having their wedding tackle inspected by the MO (who was having trouble seeing anything as the cold had shrunk their prides and joys! LOL). Most of them being given bottles of whatever kills Crabs by a VERY unamused Sister from the Medic Centre. The Twins were only responsible, as far as I know, for giving me Scabies, which was not as bad, but still met with total disdain from the same Sister, who remarked that it would be quicker and cheaper to sheep dip the whole camp!'

'The Twins got me into so much trouble one way or another, but I was to blame most of the time for taking them to places I should not have. I remember one night at the Sailing Club when Liz insisted I introduced her to the boss *(can't remember his name off hand) and as he put his hand out to shake hers, she, in her very, very tight Hot Pants, put her hand out but at the last second dropped it and gently cupped his balls in her hand.....I nearly DIED....and he, well....just stood transfixed but smiling...lmao. Another night I was in bed in when they both came in and got into bed with me (three in a RAF single bed with metal frame is not exactly comfortable), and early in the morning the Orderly Corporal came in to give one of the guys an early call. I was like...PLEASE don't look this way.....

I met up with the Twins a few years ago and they were great, both married and settled down and looking fantastic.......God, that was a really great time with them...'

His name was Flt Lt Maskell, Al, and I dealt with that incident in the original book. Thanks mate, for that exciting insight into the weird world of 'The Twins'!

The final word on the Terrible Two goes to my old friend Bob Johnson. The last known whereabouts of The Twins was said to be in the Coventry area, source the above Al Thomas – and he should know. After returning to the UK to live after Cyprus, Bob relocated to that area of the Midlands, and at the reunion came up with this classic line:

'I'll make some enquiries, they shouldn't be that difficult to find. After all, there can't be that many 60 year-old twins tottering around in stilettos and hot pants...'. And if Bob finds them - they really can come to the next reunion!

9. JULIAN

I couldn't believe my eyes as he wandered nonchalantly into the bar: Julian Maxwell Richman-Broadbridge. Of course, I had adapted his name in FTOAS, although anyone who had known Julian would know it was him from my thinly-disguised description and words. The chapter I wrote about him has probably caused more interest from people who didn't know the man than any others: mean, moody, magnificent in his ways, his dress and of course his weird 'bedspace'.

When I first tried to spread the net with the book and find a few old friends from those great days I Googled 'Richman-Broadbridge', and to my amazement got a result. I suppose the odds are better with a name like that... But the Christian name was 'Krusha', and was something to do with a housing scheme in Hampshire but it came with an e mail address. Yes, Krusha was/is Julian's daughter, so I e mailed her, and to my delight she replied and told me Julian was alive and well, and still living in Emsworth (surprise) but unfortunately was not on e mail. Krusha said she would pass on my details to her father, but in actual fact she ended up buying a copy of FTOAS to give him as a present, see the 'Original Comments' chapter. Krusha told me she loved reading about him, and my description of Julian being 'cool', although in some ways she wasn't surprised, she said he did have that presence about him when she was growing up.

In the meantime I had also contacted Ken Patchett via Friends or Forces Reunited. Ken was not so difficult to find, and as he also still lived in Emsworth and saw Julian regularly, he also arranged to invite Julian out for us to get together again after all the years. That was during the week I came over to do the P/R concerned with the book and stayed with Martin, in September 2011. Terry Whitehead, also from Thorney days came along: he wasn't 'Up The Line', but knew all the stories and more, as he had kept in touch with Ron Eldridge who had been a regular guest at his house over the years – the net was widening…

So I hadn't see the old cool dude for over forty years, but in those days of old he had had such an effect on me that I wrote a separate chapter all about him in the book. Several people, including my literary-minded big sister Jean remarked on the chapter and complimented me on the intense detail I had put into it, so much so that they could picture Julian (I called him Justin in FTOAS) and his slightly bizarre lifestyle in those days, considering he was actually a serving airman in Her Majesty's Armed Forces. Graham Logg also remarked on it in 'Original Comments'. Over the intervening years, oh how I had wondered what had happened to this extraordinary character I had slept in the next bed to for several years all that time ago – had he changed? Actually Julian had never left the area, he had married a local girl, Irene and lived in Emsworth all his life.

In this picture from Cyprus, or is it Malta Julian is far right (no 'tache this time), with Geoff Hobbs in the middle with the bottle, anyone know who the others are?

Julian had fascinated me then, as he had most people he came into contact with: out of uniform the last thing anyone would have taken him for was a serviceman. His black curly hair was much too long, over his ears and collar and with a trendy 'Frank Zappa' moustache Julian looked like something off the Sergeant Pepper album – probably that was the intention in the late sixties. In his private bedspace area, suitably blocked off from intruders Julian's world was almost pyschedelic with its wall coverings, collages and heady atmosphere. You felt you had stepped into another world as you went in. His civilian dress was different too, very smart and modern, a la Carnaby Street it seemed, as he would slip out to wait at the bus stop, to go we knew not where. He didn't mix with the rest of us outside the camp.

Well, time had not really changed Julian. He might now be well in his late sixties going the wrong way, but he still has that same trademark look about him, that 'cool' reference his daughter Krusha mentioned and that we all knew and respected - it was definitely still there. Admittedly there were admissions of the time span, black rimmed glasses and two discreet hearing aids told their story, but it was still Julian. He seemed genuinely pleased to see us, and eager to exchange all the remembered details of those days long ago, and so we did. Julian told me that when he left the RAF he had carried out a building course as his re-settlement studies and had done that type of work ever since. In short, he was a stonemason, and was still working two to three days a week. Julian's major claim to fame appeared to be the re-pointing of the local church tower in Emsworth, he was proud of that. Yes, he had married Irene, the girl we found out he was quietly seeing way back then, they had two daughters and grandchildren. Hey, cool old Julian – a grandad!

Julian has enthusiastically attended all three reunions so far, propping up the bar and chatting happily to anyone who wants to, as in the photo. In the last line of his chapter I wrote in FTOAS it reads 'I often wonder what became of the most unlikely-looking and acting serviceman I ever saw came across'. Well now I know…

10. HARDY HERE!'

The e mail title 'HARDY HERE!' jumped into my PC inbox in late 2011 and threw me completely. You're supposed to delete any suspicious-looking emails or SPAM, but curiously I clicked on 'HARDY HERE' – and another old chapter of my life re-opened... The e mail read:

'Hi Mac! Hardy here – or should I say Linda from Hayling Island - the one you called Hardy in your book, as opposed to my friend Jane who was Laurel!' Yes, it was yet another amazing consequence, all stemming from writing FTOAS, and a chapter about two friends that Martin and I 'romanced' – such a nice way of putting it – around the 1970/71 period. By the time this latest incident happened I shouldn't have been surprised at anything, but things like that kept on coming – and thankfully they still are. The amazing events that have come out of the blue (RAF serge?) since that wonderful period of my life just blow me away.

Linda was a great sport, and she and I had gone out together for a while. We had some good fun together, while my good friend Martin and his girlfriend Jane's relationship was more intense and passionate. Because of the circumstances I described fairly thoroughly in FTOAS their relationship ended, somewhat sadly, and I said in the book that it was a pity. Martin went out with quite a few ladies in our time together on the hunt, but I would put he and Jane high on the 'well-suited-together' list. So yes, surprisingly, amazingly-again Linda told me she and Jane were still in touch with each other from all those days forty-odd years ago. Linda told me her brother Gerald, who played left back to my right back for Eastoke, the Hayling Island team Martin and I played for, had seen the article in the Portsmouth evening newspaper about the book and me, and contacted her:

'Isn't this bloke that Mac you used to go out with, Linda?' He showed her the article. Oh yes, indeed it was, so Linda bought a copy, and was astounded to find herself in the book. Again, like telephonist Jill in the opening chapter it wasn't the most complimentery description, but one thing about Linda was her sense of fun from those great days. She admitted to being 'a bit miffed' over one or two bits I wrote, but Linda said she saw the funny side of it all and laughed about it (see 'Original Book Comments Chapter Three): she was and still is a great girl.

So now we were back in touch, and all four of us agreed for the sake of old times that we should meet up again – and we did. During the week of the first reunion in 2012 we met up for lunch on Hayling Island, strangely enough not a million miles from where Jane had lived with her parents in those heady days. The 'girls' both looked well, still 'Laurel and Hardy' in build, as I had unchivalrously dubbed them. Linda had never married or had children but was happy in a long-standing relationship, and Jane was a single Mum with an adult daughter she lived with. We all laughed heartily at the things we had got up to, like the parties at Jane's house, 'Bridge over Troubled Water*', skinny-dipping amongst midnight fishermen on the beach, all four of us ending up naked in Jane's Mini. The mammaries – I mean the memories came flooding back as we exchanged notes:

Amusingly they both recalled going to Simon and Laura Turpitts' wedding, as per the previous pictures, when I was the Best Man. By this time Martin was re-united with Pat, lately returned from Bermuda as detailed in the FTOAS chapter. In the picture at the top blonde Linda is middle back between Spanner (who looks quite human!) and Al Thomas, Jane is to Al's right. With his back to the camera, Mark Rowe is turning round. On the bottom picture at the back are Martin and Pat, I think it's Russ Brockbank turning round to the camera. Haven't got a clue who the rest are, any ideas, anyone?

It was Linda and Jane particularly who had nick-named their adjacent land mass to Hayling as 'Horney Island': Martin and I loved that one, we'd never heard it before – how apt with 2,000 lusty young lads living there! Jane said she remembered me from being quiet, polite and well-mannered in those days – a far cry from today... Over lunch Linda hugely embarrassed me by reminding me of a certain job she had blowing my... erm... mind or otherwise, so to speak, an activity I was very interested in at the time (I'm nearly over it, today). When Linda rather loudly reminded me about it the lady in the far corner of the pub lounge coughed, but I think she had a tickle in her throat. Linda said she was very nervous about the oral operation, as she was not sure whether you could become pregnant that way. She also reminded me how I 'wimped-out' at the taste of her Dad's mind and throat-blowing Sunday lunchtime curry which I attended: all very true....

After a great couple of hours, unbelievably

recalling those fun-filled frolics from forty years ago we all kissed goodbye and promised we would do it all again sometime – which we haven't yet. But it was such fun, and something else I never, ever dreamed would have happened – but it did! Another huge lesson in being careful what – and who - you write about, that you think will never come back, not necessarily to haunt you, but to remind (and sometimes embarrass) you and bring it all back! Martin and Jane had a good old chat too, the book had told Jane a lot about the situation at the time – if you want to know more about that – ask Martin...

*Confession time: Simon & Garfunkel's 'Bridge over Troubled Water' fabulous 1970 album really hit the spot in those days, I think it still holds 'records' for being in the charts for ages. It was Martin's present to Jane on her birthday, she still has it and remembered the circumstances, and we all laughed - although we ungallantly confessed to doing the same to a few other lovelies of the day. It made a great present, I still love the album, and can recall all the tracks on it. We certainly did our bit to keep S & G's album at Number One for several months at the time!

11. BENTLEY (AND CERTAIN OTHERS...)

Excerpt from our local paper in Spain

Yes, I fooled no-one with the FTOAS chapter entitled 'Bradley' - it was of course, the remarkable Ian Bentley. Most people who were at Thorney in the late sixties and early seventies knew Ian, but like me everyone, rather rudely really, always used his surname. Ian lives in Thailand today and hasn't made any of the reunions yet, but is threatening to attend the May 9th one this year, which a) will be fantastic if he does, but b) only believe it if you see him there...

In Bentley's story from now and then there is also a third party, a good old friend of his over the years, one Derek Heard who still lives near Chichester. Derek was an air radio fairy like me, but spent all his time holding court in the 'Air Radio Servicing Bay' on the main camp, where I was initially sent when I first arrived at Thorney. That '8 til 5 Air Force' wasn't for me, and fortunately it didn't take long before I was sent 'Up The Line' to complete my education in life. But I do remember Derek and his superb sense of humour: he was the main character in the place, and a very funny guy. Unfortunately today Derek prefers not to come to the reunions, which is a great pity as he is a real character. He knows that old Thorney scene very well and could tell some funny stories. It was Derek who first heard about FTOAS, read it, and then bought his old friend Bentley a copy and sent it to him. For some strange reason Bentley was a bit miffed about the fact that I'd written that he was clumsy and accident-prone:

'Was I?' he asked Derek.

'Whaddya mean, were you? You still are!' came the instant reply. And yes, you can see from the above local newspaper report from our local paper here in Spain that, in yet another amazing development I met up with Bentley here in Spain. We had corresponded via Forces Re-united, and he had come out to stay nearby for a couple of days with an old friend here that i didn't know, prior to leaving permanently to live in Thailand.

Quite simply, in this very changeable world of today Ian Bentley has not changed at all. His somewhat chaotic lifestyle is always a bit 'nearly' or 'going to happen', i.e. not quite getting there. While writing I am not sure whether Bentley's Thai wife actually lives with him in Thailand, or in England where she prefers the lifestyle in Hampshire, and the same goes for his daughter from a previous marriage – I think. I was being interviewed by our local Spanish newspaper for the above write-up of FTOAS me back in 2012, and as I had just met up with Bentley all the facts in the report were all fresh in my mind. Later in the chapter 'Lads New Contributions' Ian has sent me a great story that details his 'Bentley-type' activities in those days.

There is also one story I have concerning Bentley, but the facts are always just round the corner from me it seems, and I can't get all the fascinating details. Bentley and Derek, and Julian R-B for that matter knew an air radio mechanic in the radio servicing bay at Thorney called Colin Scott, and his story is unbelievable. As I was the same trade as 'Scottie' you would think I would know the details but I don't and would like to know more about him, so if anyone can add anything I would like to hear it. I was only in the Radio Bay where Scottie and Derek worked for a couple of months, I think, so I didn't know the bloke at all. The fact was that Scottie worked in the back of the Radio Bay in the stores room, his own little kingdom and was responsible for all the parts, so much so that I can't really recall even what he looked like. He was apparently only around Thorney in my early days of 1967 and 1968.

Scottie was an SAC – and somehow, unbelievingly, owned an aircraft, which was called an Aeronca C2 (see picture), and he kept it somewhere at Thorney. Apparently this was an extremely basic plane built with economy in mind, the seating being a plank across the small cramped cockpit and the controls as basic as they come. Usually with his mate Derek, Scottie used to fly the aircraft at weekends, and had a reputation as a nutter and a daredevil when flying it. With Derek's dark complexion, and Scottie's apparent reputation for chasing women (despite being married) the two were known as 'Allcock and Brown'...

How he managed with permissions and things like Air Traffic Control I can't begin to imagine. Bentley had told me about once being persuaded against his will into going up with the two, somehow cramming his huge frame into the area immediately behind the plank seat with Scottie flying and Derek larking about, as usual. Without warning Scottie suddenly put the plane into a steep dive and they were hurtling straight down towards the ground. In the back Bentley thought something had gone wrong and they were about to crash; he was beside himself and braced himself for the inevitable impact when he heard Derek cackling like a machine gun as they were dive-bombing some cattle, and realised they were only messing about - as usual!

Scottie did all his own maintenance and it was said that being in charge of the (radio) stores he had managed to requisition a complete set of tools to service the aircraft. Quite what you need a torque wrench for in a Radio Bay was the source of much amusement, but that's what was bandied about in those days. I always love the unpredictable and wacky stories of what serviceman get up to, with highly unexpected and resourceful enterprises. I suppose it's only like building aircraft to escape from POW prisons in the Second World War as an example of forces ingenuity to alleviate long hours of boredom.

At last year's reunion Julian told me another story about he and Scottie flying to the Isle of Wight to an Air Display, there posing as official photographers for an aircraft magazine. It was also Julian who delivered the sad news that eventually Scottie terminally crashed the Aeronca hitting a fence somewhere near the edge of the airfield. He later apparently emigrated to Australia post-RAF to join Quantas and then crop-spraying. In the absence of any other information, here are some official details about the aircraft and a photo I gleaned from the net:

The Aeronca C-2, powered by a tiny two-cylinder engine, debuted in 1929. It was flying at its most basic—the pilot sat on a bare plywood board. The C-2 featured an unusual, almost frivolous design with an open-pod fuselage that inspired its nickname, The Flying Bathtub. The general design of the C-2 could have been inspired by Jean Roche's initial flight experiences with an American-built copy of the Santos-Dumont Demoiselle, which had a similar triangular "basic" fuselage cross-section, and wire spoked main landing gear wheels right up against the fuselage sides.Equipped with only five instruments, a stick, and rudder pedals (brakes and a heater cost extra), the C-2 was priced at a low $1,495, bringing the cost of flying down to a level that a private citizen could aspire to and perhaps reach. Aeronca sold 164 of the economical C-2s at the height of the Great Depression in 1930-1931, helping to spark the growth of private aviation in the United States. The aircraft used a triangular cross section welded steel tube fuselage, with wood wings, was fabric covered, and used wire bracing throughout.

The Aeronca C-2

Back to Bentley...... Here's an Al Thomas memory:

'I remember him one night taking an Albacore boat from the dinghy park at the Sailing Club with his only-just-met "love of the moment". In a howling gale they screamed off across the Thorney Channel to a very small kind of island just at the entrance to Langstone Harbour. He got the poor girl off the boat and said to her 'Either you deliver or I'm going to leave you here'. She did, poor girl, so he then brought her back –lol!' *(Thanks, Al...)*

I do hope Bentley makes it this year for our fourth reunion, he has tried to make it before, but hasn't. I would think most people there would remember him and have a Bentley story, Ian was very well known on the camp. He sprayed people's cars, as that was his RAF trade, and he supplemented his RAF wages by doing it in his work-bay at weekends. For me, the man has not changed one iota, we are in regular contact by email, despite him living in Thailand. Ian is one of life's great characters and a 'big' part of Thorney life from those great days. Expect him if you see him, but if he comes then you won't be able to miss him!

12. TWINKLE IN YOUR EYE....

While I was book-signing in Portsmouth I noticed a middle-aged lady come through the main door from the Commercial Road precinct outside. She looked round, saw me and came up and introduced herself. Her name was Jackie, she told me and she had seen the article about the book and me in the Portsmouth Evening News. She had come to buy a copy, and was very friendly and pleasant to talk to, and although we had never met before she talked familiarly to me of her husband's life and work in the RAF during the late sixties at Thorney. We chatted happily about those wonderful days, and the enjoyable time she and her husband had experienced in the area for a while. Jackie had picked up a copy, and when eventually someone else approached she made to go, but then asked me if I would sign it, and write a message for me. I asked if there was anything special she would like me to write. She said:

'Can you put "In memory of Brian" please, John?', to which I was a little taken aback. I simply had not realised, although in retrospect perhaps I should have, that 'Brian' was obviously not still with us, and I apologised profusely. Jackie replied that it was alright, she explained that he had died some ten years previously from one of those awful killer diseases that are still savagely about today. ones that continue to take people far too early. But bravely Jackie told me she had a good network of family and friends around to help to stop her feeling maudlin and sorry for herself for very long - which was good to hear.

But before she left she said one little thing, which I remembered and for me said, much better than I can what I tried so hard to convey in FTOAS - about the spirit of Thorney Island, 242 OCU, and all our memories of the place. It was her wonderful, dignified parting shot that got to me, and I would like it to be remembered. I have since tried to communicate it to all my fellow Thorney Exiles at subsequent reunions. Jackie said:

'John, I'm so pleased I came along today, and I'm sure I will enjoy your book. It's been great to meet you today and have a laugh. You've taken me back years, and do you know something? You have that twinkle in your eye, that same touch of fun and happiness that all you lads, including my Brian of course had in those lovely days at Thorney Island that I remember so well. Thank you so much, John'.

Well, what about that? For me, Jackie's words simply said it all... Oh, how I know what Jackie meant... When I first came back over to publicise the book, Martin and I met up for a drink with Ken Patchett, Julian Richman-Broadbridge and Terry Whitehead in the Lord Raglan pub. The buzz, the laugh, the crack was still there, and we decided there and then, in Emsworth that night that there should be a reunion of Thorney 'Exiles' - as I refer to us all.

Oh yes, the following year on May 12th 2012 at the Thorney Island Sailing Club one of the enduring memories in my life was seeing the lovely Jackie's words come true again. The magic was still there, re-kindled from that day on, as we laughed and laughed about those heady days from over forty years ago. Yes, 'that twinkle in the eye that you all had' was there, there in abundance for us all to share. That spirit is still here with us today, and will always be whenever we all get together and remember those great days at Royal Air Force Thorney Island ... past, but never forgotten.

Thanks Jackie!

13. LANDING IN HOT WATER...

In writing FTOAS I have often been complimented on my memory in being able to recall all the events I wrote about from so long ago. After he'd had a few pints Paddy Hagan told me my memory was 'very selective' and he's probably right. Anyway, he can talk, Paddy can't even remember going to Limassol that night when I nearly got he and I killed (see FTOAS chapter 25 'The Prison'). But inevitably in getting back together I have been reminded of some events I had forgotten. One such story was related back to me only at the last reunion, evoking some painful memories. This tale is not for the squeamish, so those of a nervous disposition look away now...

Pictured below is a well-known young 'rigger' lying underneath a Hercules in Bermuda, repairing a certain leaking brake unit - read all about it in FTOAS chapter 23. The picture does demonstrate the hazards of hard-working airmen – like I wasn't...

Working on the aircraft as we all did, there were plenty of older lads who had 'been around a bit'. You were naturally the target of various scary stories about the risks of the job - and sadly this one relates to piles – or hemorroids for the haristocracy - to put it politely. Often lying on your back on freezing cold miserably hard concrete underneath aircraft in all sorts of inclement weather attracts such problems...

As such one day I feared the worst had happened to me. Needless to say the pain was considerable, and, of course I had been told – nay assured that the treatment was even worse - but the problem needed addressing before it got even more painful, it might require awful surgery – according to the 'experts'!

So it was with a very heavy heart and a sore bum I reported to the Medical Officer - MO to you - one morning. He examined me and to my huge relief advised me that I had not, as feared, contracted piles, but had merely burst a blood vessel. It was probably done 'passing a member' he explained helpfully. Perhaps in retrospect it was perpetuated after trying to eat one of Linda's Dad's curries (see FTOAS chapter 'Laurel and Hardy). The MO's prescribed treatment was to take a hot bath, as hot as I could stand, morning and evening, and apply a supplied cream liberally to the affected area - and all should be well shortly.

With a now-not-so-heavy heart back and a renewed spring in my step at the block I celebrated the good news with a hot bath, anointed myself with my new friend the cream, and dutifully soothed went back to work. Now as described in the chapter '242 OCU' our crew room was the centre all things 'social' – which included such matters – and I was enquired from my good friends as to how I had fared in the sick bay. There were few secrets between us close mates, and I was well past trying to hide such inconveniences.

'It's OK;' I breezed happily. 'It's not piles – I've just burst a blood vessel.'

'Ow'd you do that then?' piped up a curious one,

'The MO said I must have done it "passing a member" he said'. This innocent remark brought the place down.

'A member of what – Parliament?' chirped up one wag. That was the cue for everyone to go round exclaiming, 'Policitians? MPs? I shittem! - and other such witticisms.

As luck would have it, the very next day we were off on detachment to Malta, a sort of three-week paid holiday in the sun. I wasn't going to miss that, lots of fun and frivolity guaranteed, paid to piss it up and visit places you shouldn't. From memory the trip in the noisy and very uncomfortable Herc took about six hours, and when we landed at Luqa airport we were split into three shifts. This wonderful arrangement meant you worked one day shift, then the following night, then a day off - effectively one day on, two days off. 'Nights' were quite light, going on shift at four thirty in the afternoon to relieve the day shift, but you were usually finished by eight or nine, so spirits were high (and they were very cheap in Malta, especially the NAAFI).

When we landed in Malta one shift had to stay and service the four aircraft we had flown there in, but not my shift, so we repaired to our billets, our quarters where we would be sleeping for the next three weeks. The accommodation was old, but sleeping six to a room was not bad, at our worst at Thorney on our home base it was eighteen to a room, although these were never full.

In our room we got changed and discussed how early to hit the NAAFI bar, where the popular drink was double Rum and Coke, which cost the princely sum of sixpence in old money, a single tot of rum being tuppence as was a coke. Some were for attacking the bar as soon as it opened in twenty minutes time, but it had been a long flight, and personally I relaxed on my bed, no hurry.

It was typically hot and sweaty in Malta, and I suddenly remembered I had a medical condition that required treatment. I remembered from previous visits that the washing and cleaning facilities of our billets were old-fashioned but effective, so I took myself off there. There was a very large bathroom with an equally large ancient bath, the actual plumbing was a curious shade of green where the copper pipes had corroded.

'Hot!' the MO had stressed back in the UK, 'as hot as you can stand.' I can take an order and dutifully ran myself a bath, the very hot steaming water cascading in rapidly. It was over six inches deep before I turned it off. I stripped off and gingerly stood in the water, where my feet went bright red with the heat. Gripping the top of the cold tap firmly in my hand I began to lower myself backwards, determined to carry out the MO's instructions to the letter - like a good serviceman.

My mates, lounging on their beds back in the billet told me later they heard the scream as though they were actually there with me, it was a wonder they didn't hear me on the airfield. The top of the corroded tap had come off in my hand and I fell back into the scalding water. The affected area, as well as nearly everywhere else was instantly and brutally submerged, I felt like a boiled lobster.

Hey, it didn't half sort the problem out, though – I never had any trouble after that!

14. RON ELDRIDGE - SCAMS IN UNIFORM

In FTOAS I wrote a chapter called 'When I'm Cleaning Windows', where the organiser of the operation was called 'Sid Oldridge'. This, of course, fooled no-one, he was of course, Ron Eldridge, who has enthusiastically attended all three reunions so far. I went to some lengths in the book to describe Ron's debauched appearance and lifestyle at that time, so when he first re-appeared all those years later looking well, the joke was 'How comes Ron looks better at 70 then he did at 30?' Now that is a very good question, but he does, unbelievably, see above in a picture with his great mate over all the years, Terry Whitehead.

At the end of the FTOAS chapter I speculated as to where Ron had gone to and what had happened to him, no doubt using his specialist entrepreneurical skills wherever as I outlined from the Thorney days. If you would like to know the full story, get in contact with Ron and he will tell you. It's a good listen, involving America, wives, photocopying machines, pubs, a lot of money and much more, and not necessarily in that order. Ron has had a very interesting 'career' if you can describe it as that - 'life' would fit better...

However, it was his other activities while in uniform at Thorney which always interested me, as per the window cleaning operation he oversaw that I was directly involved in. I fully accept that my illustrious five years' service was brief in comparison to most others, but the role of men in uniform carrying out extra-curricular activities in service of the Queen has always fascinated me.

So last year before the third reunion Martin, Geordie Woods and I had a meal with Ron, and I made some notes during our conversation. Here are some of Ron's 'activities' during those wonderful Thorney years that I recorded. N.B See also later below Al Thomas's helpful notes on the subject, as a corporal in the overworked-not Nav Insts section Ron was Al's boss for a good while – and Al knew Ron as well as anyone in those days and tells a good tale or three.

'SOUTHERN DIRECT REMOVALS' - there was apparently a good market in physically moving RAF personnel and their families around the UK when they were posted. Ron easily acquired the letterhead of a legitimate removal firm, copied & altered the letter-heading to read 'SOUTHERN DIRECT REMOVAL SERVICES'. When a move was pending the RAF required three removal quotes, the cheapest getting the job. Two quotes from obtained legitimate removal companies were sought, plus a new, cheaper Southern Direct estimate was also supplied, which naturally got the job, surprise!. Van and men hired, job done, the RAF paid, and a percentage given back to the 'customer', who was always in on the scam: net result everyone happy...

'MR SPICY PICKLES' - a newspaper advert for an area distributor for Mr Spicy Pickles was answered by Ron. The said pickles were sold and distributed in the area around Thorney to cafes, caterers, fish & chip shops, and, inevitably pubs in the area. The only trouble with the latter was that any earnings had to be weighed off against drinking in those establishments - which of course came naturally to Ron and his helpful 'staff'.

'**BARTED ENTERPRISES'** – a Roulette wheel was bought and a gambling syndicate was set up in the block. Our friends- not the RAF police got wind of this and raided the scene, but due to a timely tip-off an elaborate system of chips had already been introduced where no money appeared to be changing hands. It merely looked like it wasn't, ie an innocent game played amongst friends. All monies were exchanged later changing the chips, so all OK, everybody happy.

'SPREADEAGLE WINDOW CLEANING SERVICES' - as well as my small part in Ron's operation, this was actually much bigger than the Married Quarters one which I wrote about in FTOAS: there were a lot of civilian contracts as well. I wrote how Ron had borrowed the ladders Julian and I used, but see Al Thomas's hilarious reminiscences involving the use of a ladder which was so warped you had to start climbing it with your back to the wall which eventually turned 180 degrees by the time you got to the top!

'HOME DECORATORS' – houses painted inside and out, in a similar operation to window cleaning.

'CAR WASH' - Ron had a civilian mate who owned a car wash business. As water was expensive and the biggest overhead, behind the premises Ron and his lads found a manhole, dug down and connected the garage directly to the mains water. It probably still is...

The following story is direct from Ron himself: 'there was one very good earner that I can tell you about and it was at Scampton. In the Mess foyer we had a newspaper kiosk selling all sorts. I became his supplier of assorted writing items: pens, biros, pencils etc. These I purchased via an advert in Exchange and Mart which I bought from him - it paid for a good few pints. I have some other stories from there but you could not print them.'

One personal memory I have from our time at Thorney was Ron telling me about from those 'Scam'pton days, involving him was 'helping' a civilian man who ran a dance hall on the camp. A double ticket racket ran which involved the public buying a ticket at the door; the punters had to then move upstairs where at a second door into the dance floor their ticket was ripped in half and one half retained by the 'checker'. Every so often this doorman would take a number of these half tickets back to the outer door where they would be sold to new customers. The organiser couldn't work out why the place was packed but he didn't seem to have all the money he expected. Ron knew though...

Al (Damian) Thomas's stories about Ron

I am flattered that Ron named his son after me, we were pretty close as he was my immediate Corporal and helped me a lot in many ways - like coming to my help when I set fire to the E&I Bay trying to make a bubble lamp with methylated spirit and OM16 in a Naafi Coffee jar with a small spirit burner under it - it was going well until the jar cracked all around the bottom and sent meths and oil over the flame which strangely set fire to the fucking room - OMG, and even worse, MY brown Lab Coat, which I ended up saving just the double stitched seams! Thankfully, Ron had a word with my WO, W.O Barsby who almost casually looked at the blackened room and said, "Just get the place up to AOC Standard by 17.00" which was fine, except it was 14.00 and I had not even started.

We also spent a lot of time doing his entrepenurial exploits , like painting a HUGE block of flats at West Wittering with no more than a ladder I have never seen the length of since. You had to start climbing with your back to the wall as the twist in the warped ladder eventually brought you back round to the right place facing the work!

I went up to Fleet with him one weekend as he had a job to do for one of his shady garage mates, we were supposed to plumb in a car wash to the mains, but his idea of tapping into the main was to put a friggin great hole in it with a pickaxe! What fun. Then there was Mr Spicy Pickles, the Window cleaning, Furniture Removals, the Line Tea Bar and lots more. Then there was carrying him from bar to bar down The Gut in Malta as his legs refused to work as he was soooooo pissed - but he could still drink. And of course there was the sailing, he used to crew for Russ Brockbank and I crewed for Sam Bott and we were always in a competition to see who came first. Me and Sam mostly!

(Ron is one of the great characters in our midst. It's great that he hasn't changed at all, still delivering eggs in a van somewhere in Staffordshire. He assures me it's a 'good little number' – I bet it is – cheers Ron, Ed Mac!

15. PETE'S STORIES

Malta c.1968. The ground crew football team who played the aircrew (I think we whacked 'em!)

Back row left to right: Errol MacBean, ? , Graham Logg, John Mac, Dave Walker, Pete Stevens
Front row Spanner George, (the young!) Pete Cox, Tony Richardson, ? and ?

I am indebted to Pete Cox and his lovely wife Brenda who took the trouble to come into the Chichester Waterstone's store on that day, September 11th 2011 to see me and buy a book. They had heard the BBC Radio Solent interview, and made it their business to come and see me – how kind, but that is a very good description of the two of them in life today. They have done some serious representation of Royal Air Force Thorney Island and themselves many times since the station closed in 1975. Pete served his time in many places over the world, he is a credit to himself- and a good man.

When I invited contributions from any Thorney exiles, Pete took me up on it, so much so that I have readily awarded him a chapter of his own. As you can see, I've called it 'Pete's stories'. His accounts are varied, interesting, and not without some challenging and dare I say controversial subjects and opinions. Personally I consider myself lucky he didn't recount the 'Where's the Radio Fairy' story, no doubt remembered from a number of cold, murky mornings up on the airfield when Pete was in charge of the early morning shift – and he often wondered where the missing airman was.

I know where he was... Pete does have one anti-Fairy story though, which could only come from a hard-working rigger, while getting his own back for once. I was indeed one of those in my trade as a Fairy who had the skin taken off his smooth hands when trying to 'bowl' a Herc mainwheel along the pan to the unconcealed delight of the riggers - and that was in the white-hot heat of El Adem... My deep respect for riggers and their lot is always immense – after all my best mate was/is one, and I used to help him finish early on nights, so we could then go out on the razz!

Here's Pete's stories in his own words:

RAF Thorney Island Smuggling Incident.

As a Corporal airframe fitter I became involved in a very difficult situation in about 1969. The problem involved HM Customs Officers and nearly resulted in the Station losing the 'Duty Free' allowance when returning from overseas detachments. This occurred when four Hercules had returned from detachment to El Adam in Libya. I was not on the detachment but was given the task of being in charge of the towing crew to move the aircraft to their normal parking bays after being 'cleared' by Customs Officers. The aircraft landed at half hour intervals and were marshalled onto the special 'customs area' and then the engines were shut down. Once the passengers and crew had left the aircraft and the Customs Officers had checked the aircraft inside they then gave us clearance to tow the aircraft away before the next aircraft arrived. On this occasion we had moved three of the four aircraft and parked them in their normal parking bays. We had the towing arm and the towing vehicle connected to the last aircraft and I was waiting for the clearance. However, one of the Customs Officers had noticed a 'bulge' in the soundproofing blanket material at the rear of the aircraft. He prodded around at it and then asked us to remove the soundproofing blanket. We did as he asked and found that the 'bulge' was a packet of 200 cigarettes sticking out and there were more packets also hidden nearby. All we could do now was to help the Customs Officers by removing soundproofing and we started to make a pile of many similar packets on the floor of the ramp. The Customs Officers then asked for the other three aircraft to be 'locked up' and 'impounded' so that could also be checked again once this particular aircraft was completed. The rest of my team and myself tried to be as helpful as possible with the Custom Officers during the incident to try to soften the obvious back lash that was going to result afterwards.

By now the Station Commander had been notified that some smuggling had taken place and he was very angry and requested that all the personnel from that detachment by recalled so that he could speak to them. In the meantime, we carried on assisting the Customs Officers on all four aircraft and a similar amount of packets of cigarettes were found on each aircraft. The Customs Officers were also considering how many other places could be used to hide similar packets and even asked us to lift up the floor panels. However, we assured them that there were so many screws holding the floor panels down that it would not be practical to stow anything underneath and the floor was also heated by hot air, so they accepted our explanation. Finally, all the many packets were taken to the Chief Customs Office so the Station Commander could see them and discuss the situation with the Chief Customs Officer. The Station Commander then addressed all the people who were on the detachment, explained his displeasure and asked for those involved to step forward. Luckily, those responsible did voluntarily step forward and were 'interviewed' by the Station Commander and they were then disciplined. Had they not done so then the complete Station would have lost its right to 'Duty Free' allowance for some considerable time.   The situation was very tense and for some time the Customs Officers spent longer when checking the aircraft that had returned from detachments overseas until normality was finally resumed and trust was established again.

<u>Thorney makes the TV News.</u>

An interesting situation that I remember happened in about mid 1968 when a Search and Rescue (SAR) Whirlwind helicopter that was based at RAF Thorney Island had an engine problem.   The engine failed when the pilot was practicing hovering over a mud bank between Thorney Island and Hayling Island.   Luckily the tide had recently 'gone out' and the aircraft dropped onto the mud bank and stuck in the mud.   The pilot told air traffic control of his problem and the other SAR Whirlwind was sent to rescue the pilot and crewman.   After that a plan was put into place to recover the 'bright yellow' Whirlwind before the tide came back in to swamp the aircraft.   Although our work area didn't cover the SAR flight, on this occasion they needed extra manpower to help them achieve the task. As our line huts were the closest to the area where the helicopter was stranded then we supplied the first people to help.   As I had some wellingtons and a water proof suit I was one of the first to be flown out to the nearby mud bank in the other SAR Whirlwind.   My task was to dig the mud from around one of the front undercarriage legs with a spade and another chap had the task with the other front leg.   We found it quite easy to dig the first spade full but the next one down was harder mud and in trying to lift it resulted in our wellington being forced downwards into the mud. Then, as we tried to get our welly's out we only succeeded in putting more mud back down the hole that we had dug. Hence we then had to start again and we tried to work out a way of achieving the task. Whilst we were trying to complete our task the helicopter ground crew members were removing the rotor blades and radios to lighten the load. As we all continued to work a hovercraft from the Inter Service Hovercraft Trials Unit based at HMS Daedulas, Lee-on-the Solent came over the mud from the sea to help us. The rotor blades, radios and other loose equipment were then loaded on to the hovercraft and it departed back over the mud to find a slip way to move up onto our airfield to off load the equipment. Meanwhile, some wooden pallets were brought out in the other Whirlwind for people to stand on and there was also some more manpower to replace us so we could have a break. Therefore, our replacement manpower did not get so muddy!!!

Eventually the Whirlwind was in a position to be air lifted and to achieve this function a Westland Sea King helicopter, on trials from RAF Boscombe Down, was sent with the appropriate lifting equipment. A lifting ring was secured to the main rotor head of the Whirlwind and the Sea King hovered over the aircraft while a volunteer hooked up the lifting sling. Once everyone was clear the Sea King pilot started to lift the Whirlwind and eventually it became unstuck from the mud. Then the load was moved forward until it was moved over the sea wall and was then lowered safely onto an aircraft parking bay on the airfield. Once the Sea King arrived, to witness the event, a BBC helicopter on one side and an ITV helicopter the other side filmed the airlifting event for the TV news. So RAF Thorney Island was famous that evening on the TV News and in the Newspapers. Fortunately the Whirlwind was not badly damaged and was soon repaired and put back into service. The RAF Thorney Island Station Commander was very pleased and donated a barrel of beer to those who helped. However, I didn't get any beer (shame) as, once I had washed the mud off my boots and clothing, I had been re-employed on another job on a Hercules before the recovery task had finished. For me it was nice to get up close to a Whirlwind helicopter again as I had previously worked on the type in the jungles of Borneo two years before. The teamwork of all elements meant a job well done as we beat the tide and the aircraft was saved.

Don't trust the Fairies.

With regards to detachments several situations remain long in my memory. One such detachment was to RAF El Adem in Libya and the particular incident involved the Radio tradesmen of the shift that I was working on at the time. On the first day of the detachment the electrical power set that we had taken with us on the aircraft had overheated and broken down. Therefore, to achieve electrical power on the Hercules aircraft the Gas Turbine Compressor (GTC) had to be operated to allow for electrical and other system functional tests. On this occasion, the Radio tradesmen had a problem with the High Frequency (HF) Radio system on one of the Hercules. As I was qualified to operate the GTC they asked me if I would help them by running it so that they could carry out some functional checks to try to find the fault and hence fix it. We went out to the aircraft at about 10.00 am and I started the GCT and gave them electrical power. Then for two hours the Radio tradesmen operated switches, removed 'black radio boxes', changed 'black radio boxes' and looked at wiring diagrams but could not make the HF Radio system work. I just sat in the pilot's seat monitoring the GTC and the other systems that were operating whilst they struggled. As mid day approached I reminded the Radio tradesmen that it was nearly lunch time so we agreed that I could shut the GTC and systems down. We walked back into our line hut offices together and as I was keen to find out more about their problem I went with them to see the Radio Sgt. who was taking over on the afternoon shift. The Radio tradesmen then explained to the Sgt. what they had been doing and the fact that they could not make the HF Radio work. Straight away the Sgt. said that the HF Radio would not work using the GTC as it did not power the 'electrical bus bar' that the HF Radio was connected to and therefore, it required an aircraft engine to be 'run' to get electrical power. That meant that I had wasted my time for two hours and I have never trusted the Radio tradesmen since. In addition, I made sure that I had a better understanding of the aircraft's power supplies on aircraft that I was working on, after that experience, so that I would not get caught out again. At the end of the same detachment the same Radio tradesmen were helping us Airframe tradesmen load up the aircraft with the spare parts boxes and equipment. One of them we trusted to 'roll' a Hercules main wheel out to the aircraft which was quite easy as there was a down hill slope. The wheel and tyre assembly being about 4½ foot high and about 2 foot wide and very heavy. An Airframe tradesman could control the wheel assembly with ease. However, after we had started our 'helpful' Radio man off he started to lose control of the wheel and it gained in speed and was heading straight for a Vulcan 'V' Bomber parked nearby. The Vulcan Crew Chief was not amused and was frantically waving him away, much to our amusement. Before the wheel hit the Vulcan our Radio man managed to stop it and push it over onto the ground. That meant that three of us Airframe chaps now had to help him lift it up again and guide it to our Hercules ready to be loaded. Blooming fairies!!!

Berlin detachment.

In October 1969 or 1970 we suddenly had a change of location for the night flying detachment from our normal Mediterranean area to two RAF Bases in Germany for three weeks. Two Hercules aircraft went to RAF Wildenwrath and two Hercules went to RAF Gatow in Berlin with both detachments having Ground Crew and equipment. I was lucky enough to be on the Berlin detachment, which was quite an experience as Berlin at that time was divided by the 'Berlin Wall' and Germany was also divided. Quite why we were sent to those locations I will never know but it may have been for political reasons as our Berlin detachment made the front page of 'The Times'. The Newspaper report stated that the East German Government were not happy about RAF Transport aircraft 'buzzing' the Berlin air border around West Berlin. To those of us there it was quite funny because for the full three weeks from 8.00 am until 10.00 am a Chipmunk aircraft would fly doing 'circuits and bumps' on the runway at RAF Gatow. Then from 10.00 am until 2.00 pm one of our Hercules aircraft would do the same and land and change Crews at midday. From 2.00 pm until 4.00 pm a Pembroke aircraft would take over and continue the flying training. After that, from 4.00 pm until 10.00 pm, both of our Hercules would carryout their night flying training and land at regular intervals to change Crews.

The reason for the East German complaint was because each RAF aircraft was being monitored by the East German air traffic controllers to ensure that they did not stray into their airspace. They could handle aircraft taking off and landing and using the air lanes in and out of Berlin but were upset that we were 'taking the mickey' by flying round and round all day long and going nowhere. Typical of the RAF - by using a system to test the opposition to see how they could cope with the situation.

I had a flight in one of the Hercules afternoon sessions and was able to go into the cockpit during the 'roller landings' on the runway at RAF Gatow. To take some photos during the landing run I was sat on the top bunk at the rear of the cockpit with my feet braced against the galley wall and with my head looking out of the astrodome.

My shoulders were braced against the astrodome structure and I was able to see over the top of the cockpit and look down towards the runway. I then took a series of photos as we flew towards the runway but as we landed there was a bit of a bump and the camera dropped and I took a photo of the rubber seal around the astrodome rather than the runway in front.

I noted that later in the life of the Hercules the astrodome hatches were removed and replaced by a standard escape hatch because of fears that they could fail when the aircraft was pressurised. The reason that the RAF requested an astrodome is because the Hastings and Beverly aircraft had them and they were very useful. However, the Hastings and Beverly were not pressurised so did not have a problem. When the Hercules fleet started to be modified for 'in flight refuelling' then the astrodome hatches were refitted again to give good vision during the refuelling operation.

During our time off at the one of the weekends we were given a conducted coach trip around West Berlin and then through 'Checkpoint Charlie' into East Berlin. The four power agreement between the UK, France, the USA and the Russians allowed for Service Men and Women to visit each other's Sectors of Berlin whilst in uniform and off duty. Typical of the British as if it was allowed then we would do it, whereas the Russian did not let their troops have the same opportunities when off duty.

The difference between East and West Berlin was so

noticeable at that time with West Berlin being full of shops with adverts and lighting normally found in western towns and cities.   However, in East Berlin the shops were just basic with no prices on show and with not much stock in the shops and no adverts.   If the shop was a tailors shop then it might have a couple of dummies in the window and that was about it.   The people on the West side looked happy and on the East looked very sad and it is understandable why many tried to escape over 'the wall' before 'the wall' came down and the two sides of Germany were reunited again.

Whilst on the coach trip we were able to see the Brandenburg Gate from both sides as it was part of the wall on the dividing line and we could see the East German troops on guard duty.   During our tour we were taken to a very large Russian War Memorial Park and we were able to walk within the Park.   However, all the time that our party was within the Park we were being watched by several East German police who were walking along the edge of the Park behind the trees.   I certainly made sure that I remained with the main group of our party as I didn't want to become separated and get carried off by the East German police.

The East German 'Tomb of the Unknown Warrior' was another attraction that we saw with two East German Guards on duty in front of the building.   During each change of the Guard a large oak door on the barracks near the Memorial would open and a Corporal would march the new Guard along the pavement and up to the Memorial and then march the old Guard back again.   Whilst on duty in front of the Memorial one of the Guards would operate a buzzer switch with his foot and on the sound of the buzzer the two Guards would change arms with their rifles. While we were there this worked well but it didn't go so well when the other half of our detachment went. On this occasion the Guard with the buzzer switch was not standing in the correct place to operate the switch and our RAF lads could see his problem and were 'taking the mickey' and laughing at the Guard. Meanwhile, the other Guard is displeased with his mate as he wanted to change arms as his arm was aching and he couldn't move until his mate operated the buzzer. Service humour is one thing but to laugh at and take the mickey out of an East German guard when he has a gun and you are on his side of the border seemed a bit risky to me.

When it was time for us to go home we had a problem with the aircraft that we were due to fly in as the day before we found that we had a hydraulic leak from one of the brakes. As we had used all of our spares we had to have a spare brake unit flown out to us and therefore, had to wait to replace the unit until the spare arrived. The Captain of our Hercules aircraft told us that if the problem was fixed by a certain time then we would fly up the Northern air corridor and take five hours to fly back to Thorney Island. However, if me were not ready by that time then we would have to 'take off' by a certain time and have a two hour flight back to Thorney via the West air corridor before the Thorney airfield closed for the night. As none of us really wanted to fly for five hours we held the job back a bit so that we could just have the two hour option.   I remember that we had completed the job, paperwork and had everything loaded back in the aircraft with five minutes to spare.   That made everybody happy even though the Captain really wanted to gain the five hour experience of the other flight.   Hence we took the two hour flight and as the date was the 5th of November we could see the bonfires and fireworks in many places in the area as we approached the runway at Thorney Island in the dark.   Luckily, no rockets hit our aircraft as we lost height but it was a great night to fly and see the free firework display.

The experience that we gained during that Berlin detachment really indicated what the 'Cold War' was all about with the huge difference in the normal way of life between the two sides of Germany.   This also reflected in the difference between the 'Free West' and the Communist Russian influence.   It also helped me understand the situation when I was detached to West Germany later in my RAF career with Wessex helicopters.

After I retired from work, Brenda treated me to a week's holiday in Berlin in 2001, by which time the 'Berlin Wall' had been knocked down and Germany became one Country again.   The Hotel we stayed at would have been in East Berlin when the City was split in two and we were also able to both walk and drive through the Brandenburg Gate, which showed how things had changed.   The amount of new large buildings being built in the East Berlin part of the City was very noticeable to bring it to the standard of the West Sector. Thus indicating how the Russian influence had held the East Sector back from development over the years.

Magnetic influence.

Working with other aircraft trades to solve technical problems did improve my general knowledge about aircraft and give some funny situations. On one occasion one of our Hercules aircraft had a problem with the standby compass, which is similar to a compass that is used in rally cars and is fitted to aircraft as a backup to the main compass system. The problem in this case was that the standby compass was reading about 30 degrees different to the main compass system no matter which direction the aircraft was pointing.

To check the main compass system of an aircraft we used to tow the aircraft to a clear area of the airfield so that we could tow it round in a circle, a procedure that we called a 'compass swing'. As the aircraft was towed we would stop at a given heading on the aircraft main compasses and an Aircrew Navigator would stand in front of the aircraft with a ground compass on a tripod base. Then, by 'sighting' the direction of the aircraft by placing the ground compass on its tripod in line with a radio aerial on top of the cockpit roof and the centreline of the fin of the aircraft. Then the heading on the ground compass would be compared to the aircraft compass system and adjustments made or deviations noted on a special card.

However, as the problem was only with the standby compass then a simple 'compass swing' was requested by the Navigational Instrument tradesmen to try to identify the problem. To carry out the task I sat in the pilot's seat to operate the brakes and also obtain electrical power by running the gas turbine compressor GTC (a small jet engine in front of the port main wheels).

To move the aircraft we had a towing vehicle with a civilian driver and an NCO to be in charge of the towing operation. I was wearing a headset and was able to talk to the towing driver to talk him through the movements and count down 10- 9-8 etc to the position that we wanted to stop. We only moved round the normal aircraft parking area but we stopped at 90 degree intervals using the main compass system and found that the standby compass was still reading 30 degrees different each time.

After we had turned round twice with still no idea what the trouble was the civilian driver became a bit 'feed up' and took his headset off. This meant that I could not speak to him to ask him to move to the next heading. Therefore, I opened the cockpit window on my side of the aircraft so that I could shout to the driver to put his headset on again so that I could speak to him. The strange part was that when I opened the window the standby compass suddenly moved to the correct heading compared to the main compass. Then, when I shut the window the standby compass moved to the 30 degree difference again, so the problem had been found. By close inspection of the window, small burn marks were noted that the window had been struck by lightning and had therefore become magnetized. This magnetism was the cause of the standby compass misreading and was simply cured by the removal of the window and then 'degaussing' or removing the magnetism from the window in the Station electrical bay. Then, with the window refitted the standby compass read correctly and we thanked the civilian driver for his part in finding the fault (we had to keep the civilian drivers happy and interested to help the teamwork). The Nav. Instrument tradesmen also learnt a lot from that experience and so did I.

Malta mishap.

Some times not every thing goes to plan as I remember a simple main wheel change that we carried out on detachment in Malta. We were working as a team in a bit of a hurry and having changed the wheel one of the team lowered the aircraft from the wheel change jack that we were using. Unfortunately, the chap who lowered the aircraft failed to notice that the old wheel was still leaning against the side of the aircraft. Hence, as the aircraft was lowered downwards onto the wheel, the wheel pushed into the structure at the front of the wheel bay, causing a large dent. Luckily no real damage was done and it could be repaired on return to our base at Thorney. The reason for the 'hurry' was because that evening Brazil were playing in the football World Cup Final and we all wanted to see it on the tele in the NAFFI as soon as we finished work. 'More hast, less speed', was a correct phrase to use in this case and luckily our boss was not too upset at our mistake.

Thorney 1 Colerne 0.

One thing I gained from being an NCO working on aircraft was trying to treat people how you would like to be treated yourself and gaining their confidence and support to achieve team work.   In addition the importance of working 'with' the Aircrew and giving them confidence in our abilities, as their lives were in our hands.

A situation occurred one day that caused some friction between us at Thorney Island and the 'air test' Aircrew from RAF Colerne.   When one of our Hercules was due for a Minor or Major Servicing it would be flown to RAF Colerne for the work to be carried out.   Normally one of our Crews would fly the aircraft to RAF Colerne and return by road or bring back another aircraft if the was one to collect.   On this occasion the RAF Colerne 'air test' Crew delivered one of our aircraft back to us after its Servicing was completed and were then requested to take another aircraft back with them that required Servicing.   This was just a straight forward task but the 'air test' Flight Engineer made it very difficult that day.   It should be noted that before we sent an aircraft to RAF Colerne it would be washed and cleaned inside and out.   Also, all of the equipment in the cabin, such as seats, chains, tie-down fittings and other loose items would be checked to make sure that every part was located in its correct place and all parts were accounted for.   On this occasion the complete task had been carried out the previous day and all the paperwork had been signed and countersigned.   However, the 'air test' Flight Engineer was not happy with many things and I was sent out, by our shift boss, as a Corporal in charge of 3 or 4 airframe tradesmen to sort out the problems, to the Flight Engineers satisfaction. The strange part was that we had never had any complaints before from the aircraft tradesmen at RAF Colerne and we all considered that the aircraft had been prepared as it normally would have been. Therefore, we considered that the Flight Engineer was excessive in his complaints but we had to be diplomatic to get the job complete and the aircraft off to RAF Colerne.

Eventually, we managed to satisfy his requests and those of the equally difficult 'air test' Load Master and then the aircraft was ready to depart. As we had been heavily involved with the aircraft I told our shift boss that we would stay with the aircraft and also act as the starter crew until it departed. I was therefore, in charge of the starter crew and would marshal the aircraft away once the Captain was ready to taxi the aircraft.

Before the engines were started I happen to notice something that was incorrect and I pointed it out to all of my starter crew but told them to say nothing and leave the situation to me, to which they all agreed. So all four engines were started and the Load Master waved us goodbye and climbed on board and closed the door. The chocks had been removed and the aircraft was ready to taxi. The Captain gave me a wave to indicate that he was ready to move and therefore, I stood in front of the aircraft and marshalled the aircraft forward from the parking bay towards the taxiway. Normally once clear of the parking bay I would have waved the aircraft away and saluted to the Captain to say that he was clear to proceed on to the taxiway.

However, on this occasion I marshalled the aircraft out onto the taxiway and lined it up until it was in line with our Flight Commander's office and then I gave the Captain the 'Stop' sign and pointed to the nose wheel.   Very quickly the aircraft door was opened and the Load Master stepped out to see what the problem was.   I then went into the nose landing gear bay and removed the nose landing gear 'lock pin' which had a red flag attached to it. I then moved back out onto the taxiway and showed the 'lock pin' to the Captain and behind him in the cockpit was a very 'red faced' Flight Engineer who should have removed the 'lock pin' before the aircraft was started up.   I gave the 'lock pin' to the Load Master, who should have also noticed that it was still fitted and he took it back with him on to the aircraft to place it in its stowage position and he closed the door.   Thorney 1 Colerne 0.

What the Captain said to the Flight Engineer we do not know but once the door was closed again I marshalled the aircraft forward, saluted to the Captain and let them taxi away.   We then went back into the shift office and explained what had happened to our shift boss.   He fully understood our feelings and then we all had a nice cup of tea in the crew room.   'Nobody messes with the lads from Thorney' and after that we never had any trouble from anyone at RAF Colerne, strangely enough.

It should be noted that had the aircraft become air borne with the 'lock pin' fitted then the nose landing gear would not have retracted and the aircraft would have had to land again. I seem to remember that a modification was later carried out on each aircraft connecting the nose 'lock pin' and flag to the covers for the 'pitot system' on the nose to make the situation less likely to re-occur again.

However, had the experienced 'air test' Flight Engineer been a bit more lenient with us then we would have been more helpful to him. To me that's human nature and proved the point that at Thorney we always 'worked with' the 'student' Flight Engineers to help with their training and to give them confidence and trust in us as ground crew. Team work!

Dave Mosey RIP.

On the 26th October 1972 I was instructed to go to see the RAF Thorney Island Senior Engineering Officer. The Wing Commander then informed me of my new responsibilities and congratulated me on my promotion to Sergeant. I then collected my new stripes from the stores and with a set hurriedly sewn on was taken to the Sergeants Mess to be 'introduced to the Mess' by our Warrant Officer, but luckily I didn't have to buy a round of drinks, as is often the custom.

Also promoted to the rank of Sergeant on the same day as me was Dave Mosey. We had been working together as airframe Corporals on the same shift on the Hercules at

Thorney.   Dave had been posted in after a tour in Singapore and we worked well together and become friends.   However, now that both of us were Sergeants it meant that the two shifts were out of balance with the rank structure and our bosses decided to move Dave to the other shift, to even things out.   This move sounded logical, but in hind sight, it just added to Dave's problems at that particular moment in his life.   Although I worked with Dave on the aircraft I didn't have much of a link with him socially as I lived in my own house away from the base and he lived in married quarters.   However, he did confide with some of the other airframe tradesmen and NCOs' on our shift and they used to talk with him regularly.   The change of shifts therefore took that important contact with his trusted work mates away from him as he now was working with people who he didn't really know and it left him a bit isolated and lonely.

The big problem that Dave had concerned his marriage and when many, many different things added together it sadly led to him 'taking his own life' in desperation.   After Dave's untimely death those who knew him were able to piece together most of the many different things that caused Dave to be in that situation and understood how he felt to cause his actions.

At Dave's funeral at Chichester Crematorium there was a lot of anger as most people felt that the situation could and should have been avoided.   As the situation with Dave's marriage concerned another RAF man at Thorney those of us close to Dave were angry that those in authority involved did not post one of the men away from the Thorney base to sort the problem out.   In the past when this type of situation had occurred on an RAF base, within 24 hrs one of the people involved and their Family was posted out of the base and quite often to another RAF base in Scotland.   That soon sorted the problem out and allowed people to concentrate on their jobs again.

My own feeling is that Dave was let down by those in authority who could have acted more firmly and posted one of those involved to Scotland along with their Family.   By not doing that led Dave to react as he did and by then it was too late.   Sadly, the RAF lost a very good SNCO who would have completed a long career and Dave's two daughters lost a loving Dad.   He therefore, didn't see his Daughters marry or meet his Grandchildren, like most of us.

Sgt. Dave Mosey, the RAF let you down when you needed them most!   Your name will not appear on a War Memorial but you are not forgotten by you mates.   Rest in peace mate, from those who knew you.

This picture is called 'Four Riggers and a Fairy'. From the left Pete, Martin. John Eade, Steve Cash – and me, the resident Fairy.

CONCLUSION

Well, very big thanks to Pete for all his time and trouble in writing the stories, I'm sure everyone reading found them very entertaining and brought back many memories. Well done, Pete!

16. LADS CONTRIBUTIONS – 2015

Now that 'our' reunion has been running for three successful years and at the time of writing we are planning the fourth for May 9th 2015, I decided to write another up-to-date version of FTOAS, bringing the forty odd years back to life. I invited contributions from anyone who wanted to participate, and the following was the excellent result – in no particular order.

Steve Cash - *Steve and I were 'stranded' in Bermuda for a week with a certain Herc brake unit that leaked...We spent half the time there at Steve's uncle and aunt's place, who ran a house for an American millionaire. We had a ball, see FTOAS chapter ' The Bermuda Triangle'. Steve's lovely wife Sue (picture of them both below) has always been 'one of the lads' throughout all the years and it was great to meet up with them both prior to the first reunion – Ed Mac*

Hi Mac Geoff and Peggy, aka Mike and Kathy in your book, lived happily in Bermuda looking after the Castle Point Estate until retirement. They then returned to Staffordshire in the UK and Geoff continued playing golf as often as possible until he died of a heart attack, guess where? on the 18th Green of his local club, so at least he got to finish his round ! Peggy went to live with her daughter and died of natural causes several years later.

I am sure you will recall that whilst in Bermuda they had a guard dog called "Trolleybus", a really vicious b-----d Doberman Pincer. Geoff allowed it to roam the grounds of the Estate and also to discourage the locals from using the beach we are photographed on in the book, as it was private and belonged to the Estate.

Whenever we visited Geoff and Peggy we had to shout to Geoff from outside the gates to the Estate and he would come and collect us to stop "Trolleybus" from savaging us. I also remember that when we were in the house with Geoff and Peggy, if the dog came in the room it would stand in the doorway and emit the most horrendous growl. Geoff would then tell it to shut up and go out and do you remember? It never turned around and left the room, it always backed out, staring at us until it was out of sight!

I also remember a two week detachment to Malta and numerous night time visits to Straight Street (The Gut) where all the "Women of the Night" worked. My favourite place was Rosie's Bar, where the barmaid and owner was of course Rosie. Her main purpose in life besides serving beer, was to show us her tits, of course being a business woman this service did not come free, it was threepence a time and no touching. I spent well over two bob with her! All the very best from Steve & Sue.

Errol Macbean – *another great 'old' mate who comes to every reunion, one I wrote a chapter about in FTOAS, calling him 'Leroy McLaine'. I think he's forgiven me now, and Mac sent in a couple of gems as below: but in the first one I'm sure (well, nearly) he's mixing me up with someone else, although I love the writing connection!*

Errol: I'm sorry to say that being in the SNCO's mess meant that I often missed out on much of the high jinks that went on at Thorney. I do recall that on one of our earlier detachments to Luqa, Malta, we were allocated one of those small flight line buildings which were built in the local type of limestone brickwork. Some lad, probably of Maltese extract, had scratched a girl's name into the stone. It read "MARIA DELORES PECHELLI". One of ours then added "GIVES ME THE SHITS". I believe that you were responsible for that addition and, who knows, it may have been the start of your more recent writing career. I do remember that we used to chant the whole verse - in a poor Italian accent.

A certain situation comes to mind. We were really not supposed to have TVs in our rooms in the service. However some did have them, one being Syd Thorpe. He was keen to offload his black & white set and Patrick Hagan showed an interest and visited Syd's bunk for a viewing of this wonder piece of entertainment. Syd switched on the set but unfortunately although a picture appeared, there was no sound. Syd did much switching of channels and waving of the aerial etc., but still no sound! Not to be beaten by this minor temporary malfunction, in his best selling mode, Syd declared " Oh, I know what it is, this is a programme for the deaf" Quick as a flash, Hagan came back with " I suppose that if there was no picture, you would be telling me that it was a programme for the blind." I was doubled up with laughter. I don't think the sale came about on that occasion and I remember Syd's furrowed brow and Hagan's jovial accent during the exchange that added to the comedy. I was the only other person present as Syd's bunk was opposite mine in the sergeant's mess. It was the funniest thing I had witnessed, but strangely, neither Syd nor Hagan can remember that incident.

Ken Patchett's stories

Ken, of course is a good mate of Ron's, both Nav Insts and legendary drinkers, see Al Thomas's stories below, who have lived to tell the tales - and here are a couple of Kens: Ed Mac

During one period of our stay at Thorney. Ron, Terry and I used to play Killer Darts at the Railway on Sunday mornings. One Sunday following a really heavy night drinking my stomach was in turmoil. The landlady Pat's sister was staying with them and had just had a baby. I had just taken my turn at darts and I farted, and following through made a dash for the toilet. I just made it, noticed the toilet window was open and threw my soiled underpants out of the window. The following day we were again in the Railway at lunchtime and I overheard a conversation Pat was having with one of the pub regulars. " Some filthy bugger threw their dirty underpants out of the Gents toilet yesterday and they landed on the nappies on the clothes line. I bet it was one of those dirty Thorney blokes"

Here's another one. I was with a 'lady' from Emsworth and we had just been to a party. I took her home, she lived in a council house in Westbourne and we were snogging on the sofa with her parents asleep upstairs. We were well aroused and swapping tongues when she suddenly made a gagging sound, and promptly vomited over the back of the sofa. With that I got dressed quickly and made a quick exit from her house. When I eventually saw her again she said the mess was all over the wallpaper and the carpet, and her father had grounded her for a week.

Mark Rowe's memories: *John Mac comment – we have only recently managed to find Mark and he is coming to his first reunion on May 9th. I have a certain 'issue' with him, see below, gleaned from his reactions to FTOAS Chapter 29 'Gordon's Wedding Weekend'. It was Mark's parents' house we all stayed in for the action-packed wedding weekend – 'Gordon' was of course Graham Logg. Oh, and thanks Mark for a priceless comment on FTOAS Chapter 25 'The Prison'...*

Mark: 'My dad often spoke about what he encountered when we returned to their house at about 4am and all hell broke loose. First he encountered me walking around

wearing my sisters wig, then he saw you (I think it was you) sat on the toilet with your trousers around your ankles but also being sick, but Martin was kneeling in front of you catching the sick in his hands and throwing it in the sink. What a good mate!
I also remember the Prison incident with the added part of where around the side of the prison they had fans sucking air into the place and we decided to piss into these fans and everyone inside had this fine mist falling on them.

Mac speaks up vigorously in his defence – In FTOAS I wrote that despite all the drink we'd consumed that momentous day I was somehow clear-headed enough to drive us all home through all the country roads with everyone asleep, and I can remember proudly getting us all back safely, hoping everyone would behave as we were guests in Mark's parents' house. I remember and wrote about Mark's sister's wig, but I was furious when I read about the honking/toilet bit. I have always said to anyone who'd listen that Martin was a honker, a regular one, and as his best mate over the years and a non sickee,I have cleaned up more of his spew (sorry, but I must put the record straight here) than any woman he has ever been involved with. 'Shuker the Puker' I privately labelled him at the time: fortunately for us both I have always had a strong stomach. I had hangovers though, and was well known for my bad temper, especially in the early mornings. But how unfair to be wrongly accused for the 'crime' after all these years!

Al (Damian) Thomas

Oh, that Consul car on the way back from Bognor... it was a Mk1, I think. I took the wrong road, and also being pissed missed a bend and we ended up in the ditch, in a tree and stuck under one of the branches. The driver's door wouldn't open, the passenger door was in the bottom of the ditch and we had to climb out of the driver's side rear window. Then having to get towed out and drive a very battered car back to Thorney, I think the engine finally seized at the main gates. And yes, I did have a shiny black Herald.....until I put it into a gate post on the night of Simons wedding.

It was Ken Patchett who had that Austin Princess on the square, on blocks, which he used to rent out for amorous adventures.lol

Bermuda - oh my God, I hope the public NEVER find out how much we cost them there! I know i had so much fun there, one way or another. Steve's Uncle Jeff was a brillliant guy. We got stuck for a week on one occasion with a blown de-icing boot on one prop and a GTC overheat and spent most days at Jeff's at Castle Point, swimming and diving and watching the baby turtles hatch out , but getting there was a bit scary. We got a Taxi one day but the driver would only go to about 500 yards from the gates and I soon found out when I pressed the bell and a bloody big, very angry Dobermann flattened itself against the wire!

The American base, Larges and the Pigs Bar - I was with Iain Moody when we stopped there on New Years Eve and as per usual we went to the Sgts Mess where they had all drinks free all night and breakfast in the morning. Well, our crew, particularly the Loadmaster kept standing up every few minutes and toasted in the New Year in every different place in the World. The Americans thought this was really strange and very odd and sent over loads of booze, even though it was free. The Portugese waiter came and asked what drinks we wanted and the order was something like 16 drinks for our group, and he just put the last one down and was going to walk away when we asked for a second round, and eventually he was bringing 48 drinks at every round order...The next morning we were due to leave but as soon as the Boss started the first engine he shut down as he couldn't stand the noise and we stayed 3 days to recover...

The Castle Harbour Hotel, Bermuda, circa 1969

That black Triumph Herald...,hmm. After Simon's wedding I somehow ended up at the Sailing Club with the twins, and they wanted to go home at the end of the evening, but I tried to get them to stay as I was well and truly completely out of my head. Anyway, they talked me into taking them home, and as we went up the Thorney Road, do you remember where after Deeps the road went right in a sweeping bend, then left and uphill and then straight and level to the end? Well, just as we went uphill, there is a gate on the left hand side and a kind of dirt road on the right , where they used to park the fire engine on payday until the money got to accounts. Well, as we approached that area, Caz was giving me a blow job and I missed the bend (been there before) and I hit the gatepost head on and put a bloody great V dent in the bonnet, pushed the engine backwards etc etc etc.   BUT... I couldnt find her. Liz was ok in the back, sort of, but Caz had somehow ended up in the road, not badly hurt thank God, but had a pretty nasty gravel rash. They stayed the night and I cleaned Caz up and I think Ron took us back to Havant where they lived the next day.

Do you remember the day I hit the Wingco Flying's wifes' car in the lorry going down to the hangar to shut a Herc up for the night? I was taking the two tonner with, I think, Spanner and Steve down to the Hangar, along the Peri-track from The Line and as I approached the road crossing, I looked left and right...nothing there...kept going, and the back end of the lorry twitched a bit. I thought I had hit a track light, but Spanner said ' Hey,you just hit a car', and sure enough, I stopped quite quickly , looked back just in time to see a white car with one headlight rolling down the road, lol. The bad news was, Wingco Flying was on the wash pan with the SWO and some other officers... oops!

The transport section tried altering the vehicle plates in the cab from being allowed to carry 3 passengers to 2 and I had to steal the whole thing, perspex cover, authorisation plate, screws etc to prove the alteration.

Fortunately for me, one of the ATC guys had seen what happened and said she had come around the bend onto the airfield at a very fast rate and that I could not have avoided her as it was the back wheel which hit her car, so all the charges were dropped, like from what I can remember some - Driving on an unauthorised route, Driving without ATC Permission, Carrying too many passengers etc, but the GC had to do something so he revoked my permit. How did I get to be a Duty Driver - they were desperate...lol. I had my airfield driving permit revoked, lol, but at that time we had the window cleaning contract for the camp and when we went to the Officers Quarters to do the windows, some time later, I forget who went to the house first to ask for a bucket of water, but she gave him one bucket and I went back for the other and when she saw me standing waiting for it, she threw it all over me, charming I thought... lmao. Do you remember the Pan races we had in Cyprus on the towing tractor. Omg...yeah, how to piss off the WO without really tryin - but hell it was fun, looking back. It's a wonder we didn't wreck a LOT of aircraft.

Ken Patchett - One night in the NAAFI bar at a party he had so much to drink (as we all did) he turned to say something, was sick, and filled my tankard with his previously consumed alcohol (UGH).

Do you remember the Australian NAAFI manageress and the coffee machine? We (Ron Eldrige and myself) tried to get a cup of coffee but wasps had made a nest in the machine and all we got was a cup full of hot, wet wasps, so we banged on the door to get her to call the engineers. This short fat vision, dressed in a red candlewick dressing gown appeared at the door and said in her very best Aussie accent "Christ, you can't even have a shit in peace here " ... happy days.

El Adem... what a place that was......full of bloody great cockroaches, but the worst were the camels, stinking, bad-tempered things.

Cyprus ... do you remember the weekend we hired a car and ended up in Famagusta sleeping on the beach and getting fruit off the trees in a nearby plantation? We had a Fiat 128 which had a duff starter motor so had to push it to get it going...and on sand it was not that easy, lol.

Then there were the nights at Niazis Kebab restaurant in Limassol, and of course the bars in the square. Who was it we clubbed together to send to that prostitute behind the green door for his birthday treat? Was it Steve Cash? I loved Cyprus a lot, very happy memories !

Malta was another never-to-forget place, especially the Gut, Sue and I went back to Malta for a holiday when the children were younger and revisited the Gut to see what had changed - everything had, no more bars, all respectable houses now, but everything else was just about the same, still very friendly local people.

Have you ever heard from Graham Logg or Mark Rowe*? Speaking of which, Grahams wedding, the VAST amount of drinks and the comedian in that club at Great Yarmouth? When we kept hitting him with his punch lines before him - he very publicly told us to FUCK OFF... which gave him the loudest laugh of the night....lol - and the horror on Mark's Dad's face when he realised we had

DRIVEN all that way, as he was the Sgt Policeman for the whole area, Mark's Mum and Dad were really nice people.

*Al's comments were before we found Mark Rowe - see my comments above & later chapter 17 re Graham Logg - Ed Mac

Ian Bentley

Hi John - I have been trying to get round to writing this letter for weeks, I hope you had a good Christmas. I am determined to make it to the reunion this year, the only obstacle is the what to do about the dog.

I thought I would try and contribute to the new book, as you can imagine there are many stories I could tell. I think the one that sticks most vividly in my mind is a night, when Im sure it was you, me, MacFarlane and Turpitt went to the Solent Club on Hayling which was the opposite corner of the Island to the Sinah Warren. I think we all went in one car, mine I think, maybe an Austin 16. Anyway Mac and I got off with two girls, and for once I think I got the best looker, a tall blonde. They were staying in a caravan at Mengam Rye, and we were assured that we were OK for the night, so we set off for their caravan and you and Turps drove my car back to Thorney. I think we made out with these two, at least I did but at one or two in the morning, they announced that their husbands or boyfriends were on their way down and we had to get out quick. How they suddenly realised that I don't remember as there was no mobile phones back then.

So now we are at Mengam Creek, which is at least 20 miles from Thorney, and we could not call you to pick us up. Then we found a rowing boat with oars and you could see Thorney across the harbour. Me being a yachty said I could find my way across to Thorney in the dark, so we rolled up the trousers of our best suits and set off. Within minutes, we hit a mud bank and by the time we had got out to push off we were high and dry. So we were stuck there for the night until the tide came in, six hours later, freezing, in only our suits. At one point the Rescue Helicopter flew over our heads and we were that desperate we were waving the oars to attract their attention. Well, they did not see us, a good thing as we would have been in serious trouble for stealing the boat. So about mid-morning we were rowing back past all the yachts in our best suits back to Thorney.

Then there was the time we invited all the girls from the Tampax factory (aka the Guided Missile factory) in Havant to a do at Thorney, and I was late for work the next morning. My Sergeant came to wake me in the block and I was in bed with one of them, and got in some serious trouble for that. My Sergeant had no sense of humour. I'm sure Julian will remember my Sergeant coming to wake me if it was a different dorm to yours. Then they invited us to one of their houses for a return party and there was Derek Heard on the door with a set of scales, saying if you havn't got a pound and a half of bollocks you don't get in.

Hope you had a great New Year, many thanks, Ian Bentley

Clive Hall - *the picture Clive sent me captures the scene in Cyprus brilliantly, with John Emburton, Clive and of course Paddy Hagan* (rolling a fag?) all having a quiet drink or six - look at the bottles! Ed Mac*

Clive: so very sorry again cannot make the reunion this year I would like to meet up again with a few of the lads. I shared a house with like Paddy Hagan* for a year or so, last memory of him when he and his then girlfriend were around my place (after I got married) he was on the floor chasing our budgie (which couldn't fly) around. Have to say it was after a bottle of vodka had gone.

Thorney Island gave me a good start and have a lot to thank for the experience I gained there. Ended up spending over 38 years in the RAF, a lot of the time on the Herc, did time in the Falkland Islands, Ethiopia and a few other places, had 5 years living out of a suitcase flying as a Herc Ground Eng fixing it (all trades) where ever we went, have a few stories from that life! Did a tour in Sardinia which was one of the best ever, also was seconded to the Kuwait Air force as a Herc Advisor the whole family went that was pretty good for us all until it was invaded! That opens up a few tales, trying to escape out of Kuwait over the desert, wife and kids in the vehicle being shot at, arrested and spending a few months as hostages in Kuwait then Iraq.

All worked out in the end and I was able to retire at age 55, no mortgage and a good pension so feel very lucky! Please keep me on the mailing list. Would also like to buy your latest book if you could let me have details of where to buy. Regards to any that may know me at the reunion. All the very best, Clive

*No book about 242 OCU could or should be without a mention of Patrick Hagan. Quite simply Paddy has not changed one iota - I still have trouble understanding his accent, especially when he's pissed...still. In recent years Martin and I have had an evening with Paddy and John Gallagher in the week before the reunions. As the Guinness flows he gets more excited and stroppy, so yes, nothing has changed - and its great he's still around to celebrate the events, especially when I nearly got he and I killed in Cyprus (see FTOAS chapter 25 The Prison, and great comments earlier by Mark Rowe). The infamous Prison's business card is below, supplied by Chalkie Richardson.

17. Ones That Got Away - And Some Not Yet Found...

Of course, not everyone wants to stay in touch with their old Thorney Island friends - and I guess they have their reasons... Despite strenuous efforts my very good-friend-at-one-time Simon Turpitt will not respond to any of our calls to get back in touch, and that is a great pity from my point of view - and that of Al Thomas, Martin and several more, including the sailing set. Before Martin and I were mates Simon and I spent a great deal of time together, he was local to Thorney, coming from Gosport. I knew his family and we even had a holiday with his mates he went to school with, a great time had in Cornwall. I wonder if he shuns them too? Since the RAF Simon has done well in his career, becoming M/D of one company and is currently a big noise with the NHS in Sussex.

Simon met his lovely (first) wife Laura on my 21st (see FTOAS chapter 'The Mecca Run') , and they married a year later on my 22nd birthday, I was his Best Man – see the reception pictures in Chapter 10 'Hardy Here!'. They were soon posted to Gibralter, but we kept in touch. After I left in 1972 and joined the selling world, Simon followed me and even joined the same company, and worked for my Dad in the East Midlands. He didn't stay there long, and returned south to work at his brother's company, Sweetheart Plastics of Gosport. He was soon moving again with Laura, this time to Sweden where they lived for several years. They sadly split up then, and Simon and my paths began to diverge. I did meet him twice in the intervening years though, but only briefly and Simon, as ever it seemed was in a rush and didn't hang about. By then he was living with an air stewardess near Gatwick, who i understand he has now married and they have a daughter..

While trying to locate him when FTOAS first came out I found an old telephone number of Laura's Mum, I knew her parents well in the early days so I rang it, and who should answer it but Laura. Her Dad had died some years previously, but now she lives with her Mum in Waterlooville. Last year Martin and I went to see her and we had lunch. Laura had hardly changed and we had a good laugh, as ever remembering all the events of forty-odd years ago. She had given me Simon's contact details, and I had even got as far as speaking to his present wife, but sadly Simon wouldn't even come to the phone, and I was asked to ring back the next day. I can take a hint, and texted him saying 'OK, Simon, got the message - I won't bother you any more. What price old friendship eh?' It really is a great pity, because despite our close friendship, and the other good friends he had amongst our group, Simon was a proficient sailor and had many friends in that Thorney Sailing Club group and the RAF, which I didn't. A lot of those who would remember him well come to our reunions today: Russ Brockbank, John Drew and Dave Hardy to name a few: very sad...

My other failure is Graham Logg. He took some finding, but I managed it, and you can see from my efforts in chapter three, 'Original Book Comments' I succeeded well, and we corresponded by e mail for a while. Graham kindly sent me some great photos for my collection, which I treasure along with many others, and some feature in this book. But he said he couldn't make the first reunion, nor the second, and after a while he stopped e mailing altogether and I haven't had any luck since, despite my efforts. I'm planning to visit Yorkshire later this year, I have an address, sort of, and may try and pay him a visit – who knows?

If those are two who 'got away', then we still have other old friends to find. This year Ken Patchett took over this searching operation, which was very successful, in that we have now 'found' Mark Rowe, Pete Stevens, Glenn Parker and Bob Heyhoe, and it is hoped all will come to this year's reunion on May 9th - including Ian Bentley (maybe...). That would be an outstanding result, all mentioned have fond memories of Thorney and the lads. But there is still work to do for everyonel. Personally I would love to contact Tony Richardson, because although a scalie to my singlie he always made me laugh, we got on well, and we did a few detachments together. Whether Spanner is still with us is a subject discussed at many get togethers - after all I wrote a complete chapter in FTOAS all about him. He was quite a character, wasn't he, and appears in several pictures. Given his lifestyle in those days with booze, and fags especially it would be somewhat of a surprise if he's still about today - but hey, you never know.

There will inevitably be other names bandied around that we had forgotten about, who may come to light and join us, which will be great. But in the words of young Mr Grace 'You've all done very well!' in our joint efforts to get old friends back together once a year for a nostalgic chat and a laugh about those great days from so long ago. The days that we thought were gone for ever, and would never be so roundly discussed and enjoyed again. I know I never, ever thought what has happened could and did happen - but i'm so pleased (and proud) it did.

Sincere thanks to everybody who responded to my messages, and came to the reunions. You made it all happen by being there, and making this old man very happy!

John Mac 2015

John McGregor

'OWED' TO THORNEY ISLAND - OR AN RAF THORNEY ISLAND REUNION POEM

Although we didn't fight in wars

Our Thorney friendships – mine and yours

Endured through years, of time and space

to bring us back - to here – this place.

Here we all worked, we laughed, we played

we served our Queen, and plied our trade

at Thorney Island, sea of calm

this magic place, with all its charm.

Was it luck – or was it fate

took us to Thorney, made new mates

Remember how we lived and laughed

no bull, our job to keep aircraft ~

always made me laugh, we got on well, and we did a few detachments together. Whether Spanner is still with us is a subject discussed at many get togethers - after all I wrote a complete chapter in FTOAS all about him. He was quite a character, wasn't he, and appears in several pictures. Given his lifestyle in those days with booze, and fags especially it would be somewhat of a surprise if he's still about today - but hey, you never know.

There will inevitably be other names bandied around that we had forgotten about, who may come to light and join us, which will be great. But in the words of young Mr Grace 'You've all done very well!' in our joint efforts to get old friends back together once a year for a nostalgic chat and a laugh about those great days from so long ago. The days that we thought were gone for ever, and would never be so roundly discussed and enjoyed again. I know I never, ever thought what has happened could and did happen - but i'm so pleased (and proud) it did.

Sincere thanks to everybody who responded to my messages, and came to the reunions. You made it all happen by being there, and making this old man very happy!

John Mac 2015

John McGregor

'OWED' TO THORNEY ISLAND - OR AN RAF THORNEY ISLAND REUNION POEM

Although we didn't fight in wars

Our Thorney friendships – mine and yours

Endured through years, of time and space

to bring us back - to here – this place.

Here we all worked, we laughed, we played

we served our Queen, and plied our trade

at Thorney Island, sea of calm

this magic place, with all its charm.

Was it luck – or was it fate

took us to Thorney, made new mates

Remember how we lived and laughed

no bull, our job to keep aircraft ~

~ flying safe, and cure those 'snags'

and then relax with beer and fags

And laugh, and laugh at all our ways

we did our jobs, in those great days!

What is it - this old Air Force base

that made it such a special place

with all its memories, those great years

that formed our dreams, our hopes, our fears?

Last year we stood near gentle waves

remembering those now in their graves

our friends who served with us, back then

when we were all just young airmen.

More absent friends? There's still a few

some new/old friends that we once knew.

Where are they now? We want to know

our other mates, from long ago.

Hey, life is strange, we never knew

what's round the corner. Ideas grew ~

for us to meet, just once- for fun?

Look at us now, what we've begun

To meet, to greet, friendships renew

and laugh together - me and you.

We are so lucky to be here

I hope to see you all – next year…

THE END.

Fairy Tales Come True

ABOUT THE AUTHOR

John McGregor lives near Alicante in Spain with his wife, Anne and their cat Cleo. At High Pavement Grammar School in Nottingham he was taught English by the late author Stanley Middleton. After school John spent five years in the Royal Air Force as an Air Radio Mechanic and travelled the world in the Hercules aircraft he helped to service. In 1972 aged 23 John went into selling and spent the next twenty-five years with four different blue-chip companies in senior sales management positions. John ran the London Marathon in 1990, and in 1995 bought a house in Spain,

At that time John began to write for magazines and newspapers, and in 2006 embarked on an Open University course which included Creative Writing. In 2009 he wrote his first book 'Fairy Tales of an SAC' which sold over 1,500 copies and he has since published two more. In Spain John joined a lively writing circle of which he is now chairman. As a result of his book about his forces adventures John now organises an annual RAF reunion in the UK. In 2013 John finally achieved his degree in English which he regards as having finally finished his education. John's hobbies include riding an old Vespa, as he had a similar scooter in the Sixties; following and writing about football and many other subjects; counselling work and he is still working selling advertising space in the magazine he writes in. Between them John and Anne have four children and eight grandchildren who visit them often in Spain.

Made in the USA
Charleston, SC
06 April 2015